TOTA
WEIRD AND
WONDERFUL WORDS

SPANGHEW

spanghew [**spang**-hyoo] to cause a frog or toad to fly into the air. (Usually violently, from the end of a stick, although it seems as though it wouldn't ever feel gentle to the poor toad or frog!) Of obscure origin.

TOTALLY

WEIRD AND WONDERFUL WORDS

EDITED BY
Erin McKean

ILLUSTRATIONS BY
Roz Chast and Danny Shanahan

WITH FOREWORDS BY RICHARD LEDERER
AND SIMON WINCHESTER

OXFORD
UNIVERSITY PRESS

OXFORD

UNIVERSITY PRESS

Oxford University Press, Inc., publishes works that
further Oxford University's objective of excellence
in research, scholarship, and education.

Oxford New York
Auckland   Cape Town   Dar es Salaam   Hong Kong   Karachi
Kuala Lumpur   Madrid   Melbourne   Mexico City   Nairobi
New Delhi   Shanghai   Taipei   Toronto

With offices in
Argentina   Austria   Brazil   Chile   Czech Republic   France   Greece
Guatemala   Hungary   Italy   Japan   Poland   Portugal   Singapore
South Korea   Switzerland   Thailand   Turkey   Ukraine   Vietnam

Copyright © 2006 by Oxford University Press
Illustrations © Roz Chast and Danny Shanahan

First published by Oxford University Press, Inc., 2006
198 Madison Avenue, New York, NY 10016
www.oup.com
ISBN-13: 978-0-19-531212-6
ISBN-10: 0-19-531212-0

Oxford is a registered trademark of Oxford University Press

The Library of Congress has cataloged the hardcover edition as follows:

Totally weird and wonderful words / edited by Erin McKean ;
illustrations by Roz Chast and Danny Shanahan ; with forewords by
Richard Lederer and Simon Winchester.
p. cm.
Includes bibliographical references.
ISBN-13: 978-0-19-531212-6 (pbk.)

1. Vocabulary. I. McKean, Erin.
PE1449.T68 2006
428.1—dc22
2006017841

579864

Printed in the United States of America

TABLE OF CONTENTS

For Joey and Henry

E. M.

For Finnegan

D. S.

INTRODUCTION

to *Totally Weird and Wonderful Words*

It's a pleasure to have all my favorite weird and wonderful words together now, in one volume, like having the whole family over for a holiday meal. And, like a holiday meal, they've brought some friends—almost two hundred of them. (The table's a little crowded.) It's interesting to see the family likenesses—so many words about odd or outdated beliefs, about things to call things you don't have a name for, for unpleasant substances and weird objects, and for professions that nobody ever told you about on career day.

Finding new weird and wonderful words is always a pleasure—rummaging around everywhere from the dusty back rooms of dictionaries to the shiny pages of *New Scientist* magazine, as well as here and there about the Internet, where even the rarest words often have a little roadside shrine of a page or two! It's fun, not just for the weird sound combinations, the uneasy jostling of letters of the alphabet unused to such close quarters, and the obscure Greek and Latin roots taken out for an airing, but for the odd ideas, bygone beliefs, skewed perspectives, and outright shocks to the system that such words present to us. These new perspectives include the one provided by *igry* 'the way you feel when someone else does something that ought to embarrass them, but doesn't' as well as the one provided by *crack-halter* 'someone likely to strain a rope, that is, likely to die by hanging.'

Many of the words in the book have made it into my everyday vocabulary. I find plenty of *obliquangled* things, for instance; and I am often at such a loss for the right (if not the proper) noun that I have to say "hand me that *Timmy-noggy*, will you?" Seeing someone *jirble* drives me up the wall, but I love to tell people that my favorite word is (egotistically) *erinaceous*, and to explain the concept of *logodaedaly*.

Thanks are due to a great many people at OUP—primarily to Linda Robbins, Ellen Chodosh, Martin Coleman, and Cybele Tom. Thanks also to Stephen Dodson for the newest pronunciations and for many points of clarification and general improvement, not to mention outright corrections (all errors remain the property of the author), and to Francis Heaney, Elaine Malek, and Henry Alford for their contributions. I would also like to thank all those who have emailed me with suggestions and corrections to the Weird and Wonderful Word of the Day mailing list—your kind emails are gratefully received. (If you'd like to sign up for the email list, you can do so at www.oup.com.)

INTRODUCTION

to *Weird and Wonderful Words*

What makes a word weird? It would be convenient to say that it's as ineffable as whatever it is that makes art Art, but that's not quite true. Words are weird because they have odd sounds, or an abundance of syllables, or a completely gratuitous *k, j, q, z,* or *x.* Words are often weird because they mean something weird. They let you see, for as long as you care to dwell on them, some of the truly bizarre things that people have had, done, used, invented, feared, or thought.

What makes a word wonderful *is* ineffable. It has to hit you like a good joke, or a satisfying denouement, or the scent of something tantalizing in the air. It makes you want to go off on tangents, or rants, or wild goose chases. It adds something, not just to your vocabulary (since you may never even speak or write any of these wonderful words), but to your being. Like anything wonderful (to abuse etymology), it fills you with wonder. It opens vistas.

I hope that by combining the weird with the wonderful (with wonderfully weird illustrations by Roz Chast, herself ineffable) in selecting these words we have made a book of vistas and not a linguistic freakshow. There are plenty of words that are weird without being the least bit wonderful—*nectocalyx* is orthographically weird, but meaning as it does 'the swimming-bell that forms the natatory organ in many hydrozoans' it is sadly lacking on the wonder scale. There are wonderful words, such as *brio* and *luminescent,* which long familiarity has deprived of any weirdness. Finding a truly weird and wonderful word is like meeting a gorgeous person who is also a good cook and will help you move.

Tremendous thanks and credit go to Sara Hawker and Angus Stevenson, whose original promotional booklet of weird and wonderful words for Oxford in the UK sparked the idea for this book, and also to Michael Quinion for much of the original material. Quite a few of the words within are from their personal collections, for which I am most grateful (it's lovely that you can give a word away and still keep it for your own). Thanks also to Martin Coleman, for managing the project, relative pronouns, bacon, and all; Sandra Ban, for keeping our quotation marks in line; Nora Wertz, for all things designed; and Casper Grathwohl, for perseverance, enthusiasm, and number-juggling.

INTRODUCTION

to *More Weird and Wonderful Words*

In the introduction to *Weird and Wonderful Words,* I wrote:

What makes a word weird? It would be convenient to say that it's as ineffable as whatever it is that makes art Art, but that's not quite true. Words are weird because they have odd sounds, or an abundance of syllables, or a completely gratuitous *k, j, q, z,* or *x.* Words are often weird because they mean something weird. They let you see, for as long as you care to dwell on them, some of the truly bizarre things that people have had, done, used, invented, feared, or thought.

What makes a word wonderful *is* ineffable. It has to hit you like a good joke, or a satisfying denouement, or the scent of something tantalizing in the air. It makes you want to go off on tangents, or rants, or wild goose chases. It adds something, not just to your vocabulary (since you may never even speak or write any of these wonderful words), but to your being. Like anything wonderful (to abuse etymology), it fills you with wonder. It opens vistas.

There are plenty of words that are weird without being the least bit wonderful—*nectocalyx* is orthographically weird, but meaning as it does 'the swimming-bell that forms the natatory organ in many hydrozoans' it is sadly lacking on the wonder scale. There are wonderful words, such as *brio* and *luminescent*, which long familiarity has deprived of any weirdness. Finding a truly weird and wonderful word is like meeting a gorgeous person who is also a good cook and will help you move.

When I wrote those words, I'd found more than four hundred weird and wonderful words. And in this book, just a few pages from here, there are more than four hundred more. It seems (luckily for us) that weird and wonderful words are a renewable resource. The mine has not played out, nor the well dried up; new candidates for the *Weird and Wonderful* seal of approval, both ancient and newly minted, are constantly coming to light. Quite a few of the words in this book were passed along to me by folks sharing their own treasures; weird words are one of the few things that you can simultaneously give away and keep for yourself.

We've also had the good luck to be able to share these words with Danny Shanahan, who has returned them to us transformed into (and often surprisingly combined in) wonderfully twisted and bizarre cartoons.

Tremendous thanks to Martin Coleman, for managing the project (without actually making us *feel* managed), Connie Baboukis and Enid Pearsons for performing stupendous feats of orthoepy, Carol-June Cassidy for keeping a stern guiding hand on our relative pronouns, Nora Wertz for another ebullient design, and Casper Grathwohl for enthusiasm, mad accounting skillz, and sympathy.

Pronunciation note: We've added pronunciations for the words in this book, pronunciations that we hope are straightforward. The tricky bits: an underlined th is the *th* sound in *bathe*. **Boldface** indicates a stressed syllable. And, because many of these words have not been sounded by human voices for centuries, all pronunciations are for entertainment purposes only.

FOREWORD

to *Weird and Wonderful Words*

Some years ago, at a time when I wrote a weekly column in a large daily London newspaper and thus vaingloriously fancied that I had some influence over popular taste, I invented a word. It was, I thought, a rather pretty-sounding word, though, I confess, not an overly attractive creation to see. It was the word *drimmens,* and it was the name that I conjured up (on a train, chuffing through the Cotswolds, while I looked out on fields of unsullied winter white) to signify the trail of gray water that is invariably left behind on the floor when someone in gumboots comes into a warm kitchen from the snowy outside world.

I still wonder how I came up with it. Perhaps I assumed I would be roundly cursed later that night for leaving such a trail when I arrived home from the station: I can't quite remember any other motive for inventing this two-syllable confection, and for vowing to include it in the next week's column, other than that I expected to leave a trail of drimmens behind me on my way to greet my wife.

It seemed a most straightforward, unfussy kind of word. The orthography was simple, the pronunciation was uncomplicated, and the etymology—while admittedly rather more whim-based than classically constructed—seemed pleasingly neat. I think, if I remember properly, that it was probably a loose mixture of *drip* and *midden* (the former suggesting wetness and cold, the latter dirt and grayness). It was in addition deliberately set in the permanent plural, since wet kitchen boots always leave behind a piecemeal trail rather than a single print. And it had the look and feel of Old English about it—such that friends on whom I tried it expected it not to be a neologism at all, but a word already lurking somewhere deep in the bowels of the *Oxford English Dictionary,* with a string of cited uses, probably sixteenth century, and coming from some striding and booted figures like Sir Francis Drake and Sir Philip Sidney.

But in fact it isn't to be found in the *OED,* or anywhere else. Moreover, and surprisingly, not only does *drimmens* not exist, but there is no word in English that begins with the four letters *drim,* however ancient the prefix sounds. There is nothing at all, in fact, to be found in any lexicon I have consulted between *drily* and *drink*—a gap appearing in all dictionaries that yearns to be filled. Hence have I now duly, and with the persuasive benefit of many months' worth of my newspaper column, done my level best to fill it.

All, however, to no avail. I shouldn't have bothered. The word does not now exist. No one liked it enough ever to use it. It never caught on. It can hardly be said to be dead since, in truth, it never lived. I have had to reel it pathetically back into its fold, while at the same time watching enviously as ugly homunculi of words like *yomp* and *J-Lo* and *new variant CJD* stagger out into the sunlight and begin to enjoy their own full and meaningful lives in the great and noble body of the English tongue. These and a score of others from our wretched times seem to me quite horrid words; mine, on the other hand, is cute. It all seems so blessedly unfair.

But I am comforted, in reading the pages that follow, with the knowledge that in my rejection I am in excellent company. "Not quite!" the pedantic will rightly cry—for the words that Erin McKean has assembled for our pleasure do technically exist, while my unloved singleton does not. But in truth these hundreds that follow might just as well not exist either, since they are all now almost entirely unused, are by and large forgotten, and are nearly all in danger of being consigned to the same lexical scrap heap from which mine has not yet risen.

Yet what binds them to mine, I feel, is that these are all exceptionally *agreeable* words, pretty to look at and to hear, nice of definition, each a marvel of etymology and construction, and well worth saving and resurrecting. They are all to be described by a phrase that only exists in the French: they are *bons mots*, a gallimaufry of philological delights.

For who could not but love *tappen,* with which leafy plug a bear seals up his bottom for the winter; or *iotacist,* one who (see all above for a living example) indulges in excessive use of the letter *i;* or the word for that oft-encountered follower of the rural trade of horse-dissecting, a *hippotomist;* or the Scots word *waff,* which means just the *slightest touch* of illness.

Our language is a rich one indeed, the richest in creation, and a privilege to know. It is ever-changing, ever-expanding, with the current lexicon like an ever-rolling conveyor belt, moving words from invention to burial with langorous certitude. This collection of Erin McKean's pauses the belt for just a few seconds so that we may pluck from it some choice delights, and place them back at the beginning to enjoy for a while more.

Drimmens is not there, more's the pity. But *weesel* is, along with *pannage* and *choronym, angletwitch* and *empasm* and *elaqueate* and *dragoman* and some hundreds more—some of them weird, all of them wonderful, and English, every one. Read them, savor them—and once in a while, perhaps even make use of them—next time you glimpse the backside of a hibernating bear, maybe; or if you see a trail of melted snow upon a pristine kitchen floor.

—Simon Winchester

FOREWORD

to *More Weird and Wonderful Words*

When I was a boy, I played with those small winged thingumabobs that grow on—and contain the seeds of—maple trees. I glued them to my nose and watched them spin like pinwheels when I tossed them into the wind. Only as a grownup did I discover that these organic whatchamacallits do have a name—*schizocarps*. So do the uglifying fleshy growths on a turkey's face (a *snood*) and the heavy flaps on the sides of the mouths of some dogs (*flews*). So do all sorts of human body parts that you never thought had names: *canthus, cerumen, frenulum, opisthenar, philtrum, thenar, tragus, uvula,* and *vomer.*

Name givers of the past have designated the half-smoked plug of tobacco in a pipe bowl as *dottle*, the decaying matter on a forest floor as *duff*, the holder for a paper cone coffee cup a *zarf,* and the slit made when one starts to saw a piece of wood as the *kerf.*

Ever since Adam assigned names to all the animals, we human beings have managed to come up with labels for almost everything on this planet—and beyond. Many of these names are so obscure that no one except dictionary editors knows them. The rest of us are reduced to referring to these things with words that mean "that object I don't know the name for." We have managed to come up with more than thirty ways of signifying that for which we don't have a name, including *doohickey, gigamaree, thingumajog, whatchamacallit,* and, as you'll soon discover in this book, *curwhibble*. *More Weird and Wonderful Words* provides a remedy for that tongue-tangled state. It will help you fill in the semantic holes of all those doohickeys and whatchamacallits and brush bursting color onto the patches of blank space in your picture of the world.

According to the Mayan sacred book *Popol Vuh,* after the Creators had made the earth, carved it with mountains, valleys, and rivers, and covered it with vegetation, they formed the animals who would be guardians of the plant world and who would praise the Makers' names: "'Speak, then, our names, praise us, your mother, your father. Invoke, then, Huracan, Chipi-Caculha, the Heart of Heaven, the Heart of Earth, the Creator, the Maker, the Forefathers. Speak, invoke us, adore us.' But the animals only hissed and screamed and cackled. They were unable to make words, and each screamed in a different way. When the Creator and the Maker saw that it was impossible for them to talk to each other, they said: 'It is impossible for them to say the names of us, their Creators and Makers. This is not well.' As a punishment, the birds and animals were condemned to be eaten and sacrificed by others, and the Creators set out to make another creature who would be able to call their names and speak their praises. This creature was man and woman."

In biblical Genesis, we read that God said, "Let us make man in our image, after our likeness." As in the Mayan myth of creation, God bestowed upon human beings the power of language, the power to name things: "And out of the ground the Lord God formed every beast of the field, and every fowl of the air; and brought them unto Adam to see what he would call them: and whatsoever Adam called every living creature, that was the name thereof. And Adam gave names to all cattle, and to the fowl of the air, and to every beast of the field."

The human passion and power to name everything is nowhere better demonstrated than in our ability to label almost everything we encounter. Through the wabe of our word-bethumped English language gyre and gimble as many as two million words, the most Brobdingnagian vocabulary by far in the history of humankind. Such a wealth of words creates a case of inconspicuous nonconsumption. Thousands of vibrant but no longer vibrating English words lie unused in arcane crannies of huge or obscure dictionaries and end up buried in the boneyards of obsolescence. Erin McKean has spent years sweeping out the dusty corners of dictionaries. She has exhumed her weird and wonderful words from obsolete and nearly forgotten graves because in her judgment they have been untimely ripped from our vocabularies and deserve another chance to live. There are more words, Horatio, than are dreamt of in your philosophy.

You probably don't know that a single word can describe the rosy light of dawn, the cooing of doves, the art of writing in the dark, or (in the manner of Georges Simenon and Isaac Asimov) the act of continuous writing, but those words—*rosicler, roucoulement, scoteography,* and *scriptitation*—have a new home in the pages of this book. Are you, like me, a water drinker and booze shunner? Then you are, in a word, an *aquabib.* Do you, like Shaquille O'Neal and me, have large feet? You are, in another word, *scipodous.* Perhaps Macbeth and his hen-pecking, buzzard-battering lady would have lived and ended their lives less bloodily if they had known that they were both *dretched.*

Here, too, reposes a superb opportunity to insult your enemies with impunity. By creatively combining selected entries of disparagement, you can brand your nemesis a *badot battologist,* a *foisonless cumber-ground,* a *furciferous zizany*, a *balatronic hoddypeak*, a *trichechine jollux*, an *infrendiate volpone*, a *scolecophagous stafador*, a *drumbling gilly-gaupus*, or a *scelestious, roinish, uliginous drazel*.

O *impigrous, illecebrous, isangelous, leggiadrous, peramene, swasivious, viscerotonic* reader, after you have explored this book, please reread the previous paragraph to realize fully the inventive invective of which our English language is capable, and please reread this sentence to see what subtle compliments we possess the potential to bestow.

Remembrance of words past also raises the art of the euphemism to its loftiest stratum. You don't always have to call a spade a spade. That's not a double chin you sport, it's a *choller*. If you are fixated on the care and maintenance of your hair, you are not narcissistic; you are, more mysteriously and less judgmentally, *philocomal*. If you have a friend who used to share your interests but—weep weep, sob sob—no longer does, he or she evidences *ageustia*, the loss of the sense of taste. If your relatives are bugging you about your state of singlehood, explain that you are happy to be *agamous*, and they may come to share your joy.

Then there is the crackling logophony of many of the words in this book, words that tingle around the tongue, ricochet off the teeth and palate, and shoot from the mouth like a watermelon seed. You'll encounter the definitions of all these ear-rinsing words in the pages ahead, but for now simply allow yourself to be merged with the collide-o-scope of their sounds: *Bogglish. Camstairy. Flambuginous. Impluvious. Infrendiate. Jirble. Kakistocracy. Rixation. Sardoodledom. Whistness. Winx. Zizany.*

Trust me. It's not *inaniloquent morology* and *balbutiating galimatias* driveling from my fingertips massaging the keyboard when I tell you that *More Weird and Wonderful Words* demonstrates that there are lots of things and ideas in the universe that actually do have names, even though hardly anybody knows them. Spotted owls, snail darters, and whales are not the only treasures on our endangered list these days. Scores of our most colorful and precise words are on the verge of extinction after generations of service. Fortunately, these specimens of logodiversity find refuge and rejuvenation in Erin McKean's wild-word sanctuary. Lexicographers like McKean are not harmless drudges. Rather, they remind us of the unbounded generativity of our glorious, uproarious, outrageous, courageous, tremendous, stupendous, end-over-endous English language.

—Richard Lederer

TOTALLY
WEIRD AND
WONDERFUL WORDS

ablegate [**ab**-li-git] a representative of the pope who brings a newly named cardinal his insignia of office. *Ablegate* is a much more impressive title than *Hiring Manager*.

abligurition [ab-lig-yoo-**rish**-un] the spending of an unconscionable amount on food. This comes from a Latin word meaning 'to spend freely and indulgently on luxuries,' which was itself derived from another Latin word meaning 'to lick.'

abnormous [ab-**nor**-mus] a word that looks recently and slangily made up, but was in fact slangily made up in about 1742. It means 'misshapen.'

aboulia [uh-**boo**-lee-uh] the loss of will or volition, as a mental illness. It's related to a Greek word meaning 'thoughtlessness.'

abreticular [**ab**-reh-**tik**-yoo-lur] of a document, created entirely by copying and pasting from documents available on the Internet. This entry, in fact, is *abreticular*, having been created from http://open-dictionary.com/Abreticular. From the prefix *ab*- 'from' and the Latin word for 'net.'

acrasia [uh-**kray**-zhuh] the state of mind in which you act against your better judgment; lack of self-control. From a Greek word meaning 'no strength.' Another helpful and obfuscating word to hide weakness; this time good for dieters.

acroama [ak-ro-**am**-uh] oral teachings heard only by close disciples, teachings that are not written down. From a Greek word meaning 'anything heard.'

acrophony [ack-**krah**-fuh-nee] the use of a picture to communicate a sound. From Greek words meaning 'highest' and 'voice.' The initial sound or syllable of the name of the pictured object is usually the one intended.

agalaxy [ag-uh-**lack**-see] lack of milk after childbirth. This is same *galaxy* as the starry one; both come from a Greek word meaning 'milk.' Lack of milk for a child and lack of stars seem, in a mother's mind, to be equal catastrophes.

agamous [ag-uh-mus] an adjective meaning 'unmarried.' Useful for single people with nagging relatives. "I'm happy being *agamous*, really, Aunt Mabel" will have them convinced of your alternative lifestyle (not that there's anything wrong with that) and with any luck head off further inquiry. Just hope that a more motivated and worried relative doesn't skip down in the dictionary to a further meaning: 'without distinguishable sexual organs.' This much more disturbing meaning is used mostly about plants—*cryptogamous* is the word more commonly used. *Agamous* comes from a Greek word of the same meaning.

ageustia [ug-**yoo**-stee-uh] the loss of the sense of taste. Could be extended in nonmedical use for someone who used to share your interests but for some reason has now sadly morphed into someone who does not.

aginate [**adj**-uh-nate] to sell small things. The noun *aginate* would be a nice term for an online auction seller. "Oh, I'm an *aginator* on eBay, you know." The citation in the *OED* gives the gloss "He which retaileth," from 1626. From a Latin word for a part of a scale.

agiotage [**adj**-uh-tidj] maneuvering by speculators to raise or lower the price of stocks or funds. From a French word of the same spelling meaning 'stockjobbing.' The first citation given in the *OED* for this word is "Vanity and *agiotage* are to a Parisian the oxygen and hydrogen of life," by Walter Savage Landor, from his best-known work (which is not saying much), *Imaginary Conversations*.

agist [uh-**jist**] to put a public burden on private lands. Originally landholders along a coast were charged for the coastguard protecting them. This could be extended to include any tax or charge upon users of a public service. From an Old French word meaning 'to lodge.' Another meaning of the word was essentially 'to give room and board to cattle.' The *agistor* (or *agister*) was an officer of the royal forests who took charge of cattle *agisted* there and accounted for the money paid for their *agistment*.

agliff [uh-**glif**] a verb only found in the past participle as *aglifft*, meaning 'frightened.' It is related to the equally obsolete *gliff*, meaning 'to alarm.'

agnate [**ag**-nate] a relation by descent from a common male ancestor, especially on the father's side.

agogic [uh-**gah**-jick] an adjective meaning 'of or about the making of wax models.' Sadly, this word is nowhere to be found on the website of the Madame Tussaud's museums.

agonistarch [ag-uh-**nis**-tark] a person who trained combatants for games. A much more intimidating word than our modern *coach*.

agonous [**ag**-uh-nus] obviously related to *agony* and *agonize*, this word's meaning hasn't yet been watered down: it means 'struggling, engaged in mortal combat.'

agrapha [**ag**-ruh-fuh] the collective name for sayings attributed to Jesus but not recorded in the canonical Gospels. This would also be a nice collective term for those quotations that "everybody knows was said by _____" but are, in fact, sadly apocryphal, such as "Elementary, my dear Watson, elementary," (which never appears in any Holmes book but is instead found in *Psmith, Journalist* by P. G. Wodehouse!). *Agrapha* comes from a Greek word meaning 'not written.'

ainhum [**ayn**-hum] a disease in which a fibrous constriction around the base of a finger or toe leads to its spontaneous amputation. Perhaps from a Yoruba word meaning 'saw.'

alexiteric [uh-lek-si-**terr**-ik] an adjective meaning 'able to ward off contagion' or 'having the properties of an antidote.' Both rubber gloves and ipecac could be called *alexiteric*. This word comes from a Greek word meaning 'protection.'

alexithymia [ay-leks-ih-**thy**-mee-uh] a disorder in which the sufferer is unable to recognize emotions or express them.

ALOGOTROPHY

alogotrophy [al-uh-**gah**-truh-fee] excessive nutrition to any one part of the body, resulting in deformity. Like many unnerving and disturbing medical words, this one seems to be more a theory of disease than an actual condition. It comes from Greek roots meaning 'unreasonable nourishment.'

angletwitch [**ang**-guhl-twich] (also *angletouch*) an obsolete but charming word meaning 'a worm used as bait in fishing.'

anopisthograph [an-oh-**pis**-thoh-graf] something that has writing on only one side (usually paper, although you could pedantically use this for things like T-shirts or billboards). *Anopisthography* is the practice of writing on only one side of something, a policy disdained by those who know how to make that 1   2 button on the copy machine work. (*Opisthography* is the practice of writing on both sides.) From Greek words that mean 'written on the back or cover.'

antapology [ant-uh-**pah**-luh-jee] a reply to an apology. Very rare, this word deserves a wider use to describe responses to apologies such as "Well, you should be sorry!"

anthropoglot [an-**thro**-puh-glot] an animal that has a humanlike tongue, such as a parrot.

antonomasia [an-tuh-noh-**may**-zee-uh] the practice, abhorred by lawyers, of using a trademark (like *Kleenex* or *Xerox*) as a generic term. From Greek words meaning 'against' and 'to name.' If this is done often enough (and the owners of the trademark do not protest enough) the word may become generic, as happened with *thermos* and *aspirin*.

apocatastasis [a-po-kuh-**tass**-tuh-sis] the return to a previous condition. Although mostly used in astronomical and medical contexts, this would make a nice alternative to the overused *rehab*. "We've almost completed our apocatastasis; we're just waiting for the tiles we ordered from Italy."

7

ABERRANT AND
AMAZING ANATOMY

Anyone who has ever contemplated the essential humor of the belly button (*omphalodium*) or the big toe (*hallux*) would not be surprised at the number of unusual words available to describe our odd extremities and parts.

There are quite a few terms right at your fingertips. The very fingertip, the part with the fingernail, is the *metacondylus*. The fingertip, not including the nail, is the *dactylion*. The nail itself is an *unguicule*. Your *annularis*, or ring-finger, not only has a direct line to your heart, but supposedly also cures disease (thus the name *leech-finger* if you're a doctor). If you're all thumbs, perhaps you have one *pollex* too many? If you have lost a thumb, you're *murcous*. If you have one finger or toe too many (especially one on the far side of your little toe or little finger) it's a *postminimus*. Your little finger is also called your *ear-finger* or *auricular*, being the most convenient, one assumes, for investigations into the *souse*, 'ear.' The hollow of the external ear is called the *alveary*, because the wax is found there. *Alveary* comes from a Latin word meaning 'beehive.' The little flap on the inner side of the external ear is the *tragus*; it is opposite the *helix*, which is the rim of the external ear. The palm of the hand and the sole of the foot have the same name—*thenar*, which is also the name for the ball of muscle at the base of the thumb.

Your bendy parts also have good names. You may not know your ear from your *ancon* if you're unaware that your *ancon* is your elbow. The bend of the elbow itself is the *bought*. Your *oxter* is your armpit. *Knapper* for knee is a little easier to grasp, but most people don't know that the space behind the knee is called the *hough*. The kneecap has a slew of names, including *knop, rotula, rowel, shive, whirl-bone,* and *pattle-bone.* Something that bends like a knee is *geniculate*. Going from the top down on the leg, you can refer to your *coxa* or *huckle* (hip), *meros* (thigh), *hockshin* or *gambrel* (the underside of your thigh), *sparlire* (calf), *astragalus* or *coot* (ankle-bone), down to the *pterna* (heel-bone).

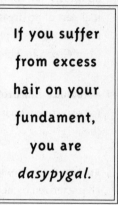

If you suffer from excess hair on your fundament, you are dasypygal.

If you're sitting down while you read this, you are using your *crupper, fud, bewscher, hurdies, crus, rass,* and *toute* to its full potential, not to mention your *crena,* 'the crease between the buttocks.' (If you suffer from excess hair on your fundament, you are *dasypygal*.)

There are all sorts of little odds and ends around the body that have good names, like the *columella,* the little flap that hangs down in the back of your throat (often called the *uvula*), and the cavity in which it hangs, the *fauces.* The blank spaces of your face, like the *glabella* (the space between your eyebrows) and the *philtrum* or *pallium* (the dent of your upper lip) should be, in most cases, *glabrous* 'smooth.' It sounds more determined to grit your *mompyns* instead of your teeth, or to stick out your *pogonion* 'most projecting part of a chin.' Quite possibly the nicest term of all, though, is *heart-spoon,* the little dent at the end of your sternum. Or it would be, if the citations for it didn't involve it being used to whet an attacker's knife.

apocrisiary [a-po-**kriz**-ee-a-ree] a person appointed to give answers. Used especially of papal nuncios, this word has a much nicer (and more impressive) sound than Public Relations Manager. It comes from a Greek word meaning 'answer.'

apoptosis [ap-ahp-**toh**-sis] the death of cells which occurs as a normal part of an organism's growth or development: a less technical term for this process is *programmed cell death*. The term *apoptosis* comes from Greek, in which it means 'falling-off.'

aproctous [uh-**prok**-tus] having no anus. Perhaps this could be used for someone who is incapable of acting like an ass, no matter how hard they try?

aprosexia [a-pro-**sex**-ee-uh] an abnormal inability to pay attention, characterized by near-complete indifference to everything (as opposed to generic, run-of-the-mill absent-mindedness). It is contrasted with *hyperprosexia*, concentration on one thing to the exclusion of everything else, and *paraprosexia*, the inability to pay attention to any one thing, caused by a constant state of distraction.

aquabib [**ack**-wuh-bib] a water drinker. Someone hated by bartenders and waiters everywhere.

aquamanile [a-kwuh-muh-**nye**-lee] or [a-kwuh-muh-**nee**-lee] a bowl or jug made in the form of an animal or bird.

architricline [ar-chee-**trik**-lin] the master of a feast. In medieval legend, *Architricline* was thought to be the name of a rich lord. It comes from Greek words meaning 'chief' and 'dining couch.'

argute [ahr-**gyoot**] or [**ahr**-gyoot] an adjective meaning 'shrewd.' Arising in the sixteenth century from a Latin word meaning 'clear or sharp,' it is a very rare word used only in scholarly or literary writing.

aristotle [a-riss-**tah**-tuhl] rhyming slang for 'bottle.' Other examples of rhyming slang include *Joe Blake,* 'a snake,' *jimmygrant,* 'an immigrant,' and *molly the monk,* 'a drunk.'

ascesis [uh-**see**-sis] the practice of self-discipline. Fittingly enough, it comes from a Greek word meaning 'to exercise.' Many people need to exert their ascesis to the utmost in order to force themselves to exercise.

aspectabund [uh-**spek**-tuh-bund] an adjective meaning 'having an expressive face.'

aspheterism [ass-**fet**-tuh-rizm] the belief that there should be no private property; a synonym for communism. This word comes from a Greek word meaning 'nothing of one's own.'

asseclist [**ass**-uh-klist] this suggestive combination of letters means 'an attendant or follower' and comes from a Latin word meaning 'to follow after.' But it alludes to so much more that it's a very satisfying word to use.

astrobleme [**ass**-truh-bleem] an eroded remnant of a large, ancient crater made by the impact of a meteorite or comet. The term comes from the Greek words for 'star' and 'wound.'

ASPECTABUND

atrabilious [at-ruh-**bil**-yuhs]   an adjective meaning 'melancholy or bad-tempered.' Used mainly in literary writing, it comes from the Latin term *atra bilis*, meaning 'black bile.' In medieval times, black bile was one of the four cardinal humors, body fluids whose relative proportions were believed to determine a person's physical and mental qualities. Black bile was thought to cause melancholy: the other three were yellow bile, phlegm, and blood, associated respectively with irascibility, calmness or stolidity, and optimism.

aucupate [**aw**-kyoo-pate] a verb meaning 'to go bird-catching.' It also can be used figuratively to mean 'to lie in wait for or hunt.' It comes from Latin words meaning 'bird' and 'catch.'

autochthon [aw-**tahk**-thuhn] a human being born from the soil where he or she lives (like the Biblical Adam). Also used as a synonym for *aborigine*, it comes from a Greek word meaning 'sprung from that land itself.'

autogeneal [aw-to-**jee**-nee-uhl] self-produced, made by yourself. This does not (yet) have a theatrical usage, but it's easy to imagine one: "In his autogeneal play, he explores themes of mania and dissolution." This word comes from a Greek word with the same meaning.

autological [aw-to-**lahj**-ih-kuhl] of an adjective, having the property that it describes. The antonym is *heterological*. Thus, the adjective *sesquipedalian* is autological, the adjective *infinitesimal* is heterological.

autophoby [aw-**tah**-fuh-bee] the fear of referring to yourself, usually manifested by the reluctance to use the pronouns *I* or *me*. This fear may be based on uncertainty about the proper pronoun to use, or come about through a pathological modesty. Autophobes are fond of using *myself* as a less-frightening replacement for the dread pronouns. "If you have questions, take them up with John or myself." "Alice and myself are going to the movies."

autoptic [aw-**tahp**-tik] an adjective meaning 'based on personal observation, eyewitness.' This word is usually used in legal contexts, as in *autoptic testimony* and *autoptic witness.*

autoschediastic [aw-to-sked-ee-**ass**-tik] done on the spur of the moment or improvised. This word comes from a Greek word meaning 'to act or speak offhand.' (As luck would have it, this entry itself was put in at the last minute.)

avetrol [av-uh-trawl] a bastard. Possibly related to a Latin word meaning 'to debauch, to corrupt,' bastards for centuries being thought of as a natural consequence of debauchery.

SLANGREL AVETROL GANGREL

BABLATRICE

...had lunch with Marjorie at the River View – the salad bar alone was worth the trip! There must have been eleven kinds of pasta salad – corkscrews; elbow macaroni; fusilli; penne – plain and the kind with those little grooves down the sides; shells – no, wait a minute, maybe they didn't have shells... NO! I REMEMBER! There WERE shells, they were just more off to the left, and the rest of the pasta salads were on the right. And the BREAD! It was out of this world!!! Pumpernickel, rye, seeded, corn bread...

bablatrice [**bab**-luh-triss] a female babbler. *Chaterestre* is another word for a talkative woman. A *leighster* is a female liar.

badot [bad-**doh**] a rare and obsolete adjective meaning 'silly.' From a French word meaning 'a gaping idler.'

baetyl [**bee**-tuhl] a sacred meteoric stone. These stones were thought to have life, and were sometimes set up underneath holy trees.

baisemain [bez-**man**] an obsolete word meaning 'a kiss on the hand,' and, by extension, 'compliments.' From a French word of the same meaning.

baithe [ba<u>the</u>] a rare and obsolete word meaning 'to agree, to consent.' From an Old Norse word meaning 'to beg.'

balatronic [bal-uh-**trah**-nik] an adjective meaning 'of or pertaining to buffoons.' The citation in the *OED* refers to "students of the balatronic dialect [who keep] an interleaved copy of the Slang Dictionary." For research purposes, only, of course. From a Latin word meaning 'babbler.'

balbutiate [bal-**byoo**-shee-ate] to stutter or stammer. From a Latin word meaning 'to stammer.' Someone who is *balbutient* is stammering. *Balbuties* is the medical term for stuttering or lisping, or, as one citation has it, "vicious pronunciation."

balistraria [ba-liss-**trair**-ee-uh] the proper name of those cross-shaped holes in the walls of fortresses and castles, through which weapons (usually crossbows, or *arbalests*) could be fired. Also, a room in which to keep your arbalests. If you're able to fire an arbalest you could be called a *balistrier*.

ballotade [bal-uh-**tayd**] a kind of jump in which a horse bends all four legs without kicking out the hind ones. (No animals were injured in the writing of this definition.) From a French word meaning 'a small ball.' Another word from this root is *ballottement*, a way of diagnosing pregnancy, where the front of the uterus is pushed suddenly and the fetus is felt to move away and back again. It would seem most pregnancies would be fairly apparent by the time this method was effective.

bandoline [**band**-uh-lin] a sticky preparation formerly used to set hair in place. From the quotations in the *OED*, it sounds like rather unpleasant stuff: "the boiled pips [of quinces] make the glutinous preparation called bandoline." The origin of the term is uncertain.

barathrum [**barr**-uh-thrum] a deep pit in Athens, into which condemned criminals were thrown to die. There are as yet no *barathrums* in Texas. Also, any pit or abyss.

bardolatry [bar-**dah**-luh-tree] a humorous term for excessive admiration of William Shakespeare, who is sometimes referred to as the *Bard* or the *Bard of Avon*. It appears to have been coined by George Bernard Shaw in the early 1900s, together with the related words *bardolater* and *bardolatrous*. *Shakespearolatry* is another word with the same meaning, but this is rarely if ever used.

barla-fumble [**bahr**-luh **fum**-ble] a call for a time-out or truce by someone who has fallen while playing or wrestling. From *parley*, 'truce.'

batie-bummil [**bay**-tee-buhm-uhl] a useless bungler. An obsolete Scottish dialect word. It is unknown whether there are more useless bunglers in Scotland than elsewhere, or—much more likely—less tolerance of them.

battologist [bat-**tah**-luh-djist] someone who repeats the same thing needlessly. From a Greek word meaning 'stammerer.'

bematist [**bee**-muh-tist] an official road-surveyor in the time of Alexander the Great. This word comes from a Greek word meaning 'to measure by paces.'

bezoar [**bee**-zor] a small hard mass that sometimes forms in the stomachs of certain animals, especially ones that chew the cud, such as goats or sheep. In former times, these lumps were believed to be an antidote for various ailments or conditions: they were either swallowed or rubbed on the affected part of the body. The term comes from a Persian word meaning 'antidote.' A *phytobezoar* is a lump formed chiefly of vegetable matter, while a *trichobezoar* is one formed chiefly of hair.

bibesy [**bib**-uh-see] an obsolete or perhaps completely invented word from Nathan Bailey's *Universal Etymological Dictionary* of 1731 meaning 'a too earnest desire after drink.' It is taken from a Latin word of Plautus, *bibesia*, meaning 'the land of drinks' or 'the drink-land.'

BEZOAR

(TRICHOBEZOAR)

bicrural [bye-**kroor**-uhl] two-legged. This word was most likely coined from Latin roots because the non-Latinate word just wasn't jargony or elevated enough. Sadly, although the word *tricrural* exists, no references were found to people running in tricrural races. Another fancy *bi-* word, with a citation from 1866, is *biduous*, meaning 'lasting for two days.' *Triduous* is not found, lending more credence to the theory that Victorians did not have three-day weekends.

bifilar [bye-**fye**-ler] having two threads or using two threads. Most modern sewing machines are *bifilar* (or even *tri-* or *quatrifilar*). Early sewing machines weren't—they were trying to reproduce mechanically *monofilar* handsewing, unsuccessfully—and it wasn't until 1833 that an American Quaker, Walter Hunt, invented the first *bifilar* sewing machine. (Unfortunately, it couldn't sew curved seams, so it wasn't a success either.)

birse [buhrs] an old Scottish word for 'bristle.' The *OED* also gives *to lick the birse*, 'to pass a small bunch of hog's bristles through the mouth—as is done on being made a 'soutar of Selkirk.' Please take my name off the list for consideration for that honor. (A *soutar* is a cobbler or shoemaker.)

blagueur [blah-**goor**] a person who talks pretentiously. From a French word, *blague*, meaning 'pretentious falsehood,' self-aggrandizing stories knowing no borders.

blandiose [bland-ee-**ohs**] an adjective to describe something that wants to be grand (or has pretensions to grandeur) but is only bland. The word was probably coined by the writer Kenneth Tynan (1927–1980) in the mid-twentieth century.

blastophthoria [blast-o-**fthor**-ee-uh] the hypothetical degeneration of germ cells (sperm cells and egg cells) supposedly caused by alcoholism.

blennorrhea [blen-uh-**ree**-uh] an unusually large secretion and discharge of mucus. You know that any word ending in *-rrhea* is bound to be unpleasant, but this one is particularly so. Something (or an unfortunate someone) who is *blennogenous* generates mucus.

blesiloquent [bleh-**sil**-oh-kwuhnt] speaking with a lisp or a stammer. From Latin words meaning 'lisping, stammering' and 'speaking.'

blive [bleev] an obsolete adverb that originally meant 'immediately, right away' but gradually came to mean 'before long, soon,' just in the same way that "I'll be there in a second" means "I hope you have something to read while you wait."

bloncket [**blahng**-kit] gray, or a light grayish blue. It comes from a French word meaning "whitish," and like many whitish things, eventually became flat-out gray.

blottesque [blah-**tesk**] (of paintings) having blots or heavy brushwork, not finely done. A combination of *blot* and the *-esque* of *grotesque*. Not, as you might imagine, a complimentary term, it was first used by John Ruskin to criticize modern painting.

bloviate [**bloh**-vee-ate] to speak in a pompous or overbearing way. This is a mock-Latin fancying-up of *blow* or *boast*. The word was made popular by President Warren G. Harding (1865–1923).

bogglish [**bahg**-glish] uncertain, doubtful, skittish. This is one of those words which, if it did not exist, would have to be invented for the pure joy of the combination of letters and sounds. How nice to be able to say, "I'll have to get back to you about that, I'm a bit *bogglish*."

bombilation [bahm-buh-**lay**-shun] a buzzing, droning, or humming sound. This word sounds as if it should be much more severe than the definition strictly allows; if you had said you were kept awake by *bombilation* all night, it seems that rubble and sirens would be expected, not just somebody's overbassed car or a neighbor's TV.

bombycinous [bom-**biss**-ih-nus] an adjective meaning 'pale yellow, like a silkworm.' From a Latin word meaning 'silken.'

bombylious [bom-**bye**-lee-uhs] buzzing like a large bee. There does not seem to be a special word for buzzing like a small bee, or even a medium-sized bee. From a Greek word for bee.

bondieuserie [bon-**dyoo**-zuh-ree] a collective term for kitschy religious ornaments or devotional objects. From the French *bon Dieu,* or 'good God,' which I expect was said like this: "Bon Dieu! We don't need another plastic Virgin Mary!"

boodge [booj] a box or container on the back of a carriage, used to carry swords (or less romantic things, like packages). The word, like carriages, is obsolete, and might be related to a French word for 'wallet.'

bordlode [**bord**-lode] a service required of tenants, particularly the duty to carry firewood from the woods to the landlord's house. This makes the requirements of co-op and condo boards seem relatively reasonable.

Bosco Pertwee [**boss**-ko-**purt**-wee] a name used to trap pretentious people who pretend to know everything—the idea is to say something like "That's a good movie, but I prefer the work of director Bosco Pertwee—don't you?" and listen to them fall all over themselves to have an opinion. A listener to Nigel Rees' BBC radio show *Quote Unquote* invented him as a service to humanity.

boukie [**boo**-kee] a flower made of fabric or leather, worn as an accessory.

bouffage [boo-**fahzh**] a filling meal. From an Old French word glossed in the *OED* with a quote from Cotgrave as 'any meat that (eaten greedily) fills the mouth, and makes the cheeks to swell; cheeke-puffing meat.'

brabbling [**brab**-ling] noisy arguing or hair-splitting. From obsolete *brabble,* to argue noisily about insignificant things.

brannigan [**bran**-ig-in] a rare word meaning 'a drinking bout, a spree or binge.' One of the citations in the *OED* is from H. L. Mencken's *American Mercury* magazine: "He may seek escape by going on prolonged crossword puzzle *brannigans*." You can sense Mencken's pleasure in contrasting a word like *brannigan* with such a sedentary occupation.

breastsummer [**bress**-uh-mer] a large beam, extending horizontally over an opening, that supports the whole weight of the wall above it. The -*summer* part of this word comes from a French word meaning 'beam,' and *breast* is often used, especially in building and nautical compounds, to mean 'support.'

breloque [bruh-**lohk**] a charm or ornament for a watch chain. This seems to have been a slightly risible thing to wear or have; the *OED* has a quote from Thackeray: "His chains and breloques…and ambrosial moustaches."

bromatology [broh-muh-**tah**-luh-jee] a treatise on food. A good word for the kind of cookbook that gives you recipes for food that is good for you, instead of for food that you actually want to eat. *Bromo-*, a Greek root meaning 'food,' is also the *bromo-* of *Bromo Seltzer*, and *bromo* on its own (no hyphen) means food that is eaten and not drunk (where does ice cream fit on this continuum?) or a preparation of chocolate. The scientific name of the cacao plant is *Theobroma cacao, theobroma* meaning 'food of the gods.'

BREASTSUMMER

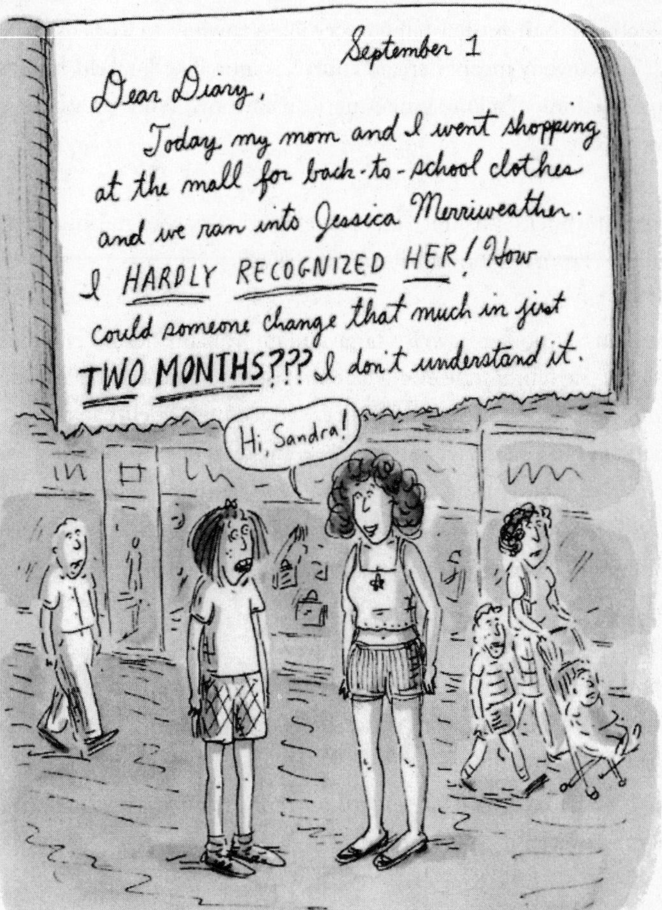

brume [**broom**] a poetic term meaning 'mist or fog.' It arose in the early nineteenth century and came from a Latin word for 'winter,' as did the adjective *brumous*, meaning 'foggy or wintry.'

bubulcitate [buh-**bull**-si-tate] to cry like a cowboy, to work as a cowboy. (The cowboy meant here, of course, is more like *cowherd*, but it's funnier to think of a lonesome American cowboy.) From a Latin word meaning 'cowherd.'

bucculent [**buck**-yuh-lunt] an obsolete and rare word meaning 'widemouthed.' From a Latin word meaning 'cheek.'

bucentaur [byoo-**sen**-tawr] a large and improbably decorated barge, often one used for a state event. The first of the name may have been the one in which the Doges of Venice pledged their fidelity to the Adriatic Sea in a marriage ceremony on the feast of the Ascension every year. A *bucentaur* is also a half-man half-ox creature.

buchette [boo-**shett**] a rare and obsolete word meaning 'a piece of firewood.'

buffard [**buff**-erd] an obsolete and rare word meaning 'a fool.' Possibly from a French word meaning 'often puffing.'

bufo [**byoo**-foh] an obsolete word meaning 'the black tincture of the alchemists.' From a Latin word meaning 'toad.'

bullimong [**bull**-uh-mung] various grains all mixed together, used for feeding cattle. By extension, any heterogenous mess.

BUBULCITATE

byhore [by-**hor**] an obsolete word meaning 'to commit adultery against.' It seems odd to the modern ear to think of adultery as something you do to someone else, instead of with someone else.

byssaceous [bi-**say**-shus] an adjective meaning 'composed of fine tangled threads.' It is usually used in botanical contexts but should be useful for incompetent knitters.

cagastrical [kuh-**gas**-tri-kuhl] an adjective used to describe diseases thought to be caused by the influence of malignant stars, which at one time or another included plague and fever. The word comes from Greek roots meaning 'evil star.'

calamistrate [ka-luh-**mis**-trate] a rare verb meaning 'to curl the hair.' This word comes from the Latin word for 'curling-iron.'

callipygian [ka-li-**pij**-ee-uhn] an adjective meaning 'having shapely buttocks.' The term comes from Greek words meaning 'beauty' and 'buttocks'; a related word is *steatopygia*, used to refer to the accumulation of large amounts of fat on the buttocks.

camorra [kuh-**mor**-uh] a secret society, usually one breaking the law. This word comes from the name of a group that was active in Naples in the nineteenth century.

campaniform [kam-**pan**-i-form] an adjective meaning 'shaped like a bell.' Since such a lot of things are bell-shaped, there are several adjectives with the same meaning, including *campanulous*, *campanulate*, and *campanular*. *Campaniliform* means 'shaped like a bell-tower or steeple.'

camstairy [kam-**stair**-ee] a Scots adjective meaning 'perverse, willful, or obstinate.' Possibly related to *cam*, 'crooked.'

canescent [kuh-**ness**-unt] hoary, grayish or dull white, like the hairs on the leaves of plants. Although this looks like it should be related to *canine*, it's from a Latin word meaning 'to grow hoary.' Perhaps it could be used to describe certain dinner-party stories, especially those related by one's spouse.

capnography [kap-**nah**-gruh-fee] the measurement of exhaled CO_2, used by anesthesiologists to monitor patients. It comes from a Greek word for 'smoke,' and -*graphy*.

caphar [kaf-**fahr**] an obsolete word for the money paid for protection by Christian merchants taking merchandise to Jerusalem. From an Arabic word meaning 'defense.'

capilotade [kap-i-loh-**tahd**] a hashed-together story. From the name of a dish made of minced veal, chicken, capon, or partridge, separated by beds of cheese.

carmagnole [kar-muh-**nyohl**] a bombastic style of writing used by journalists to report the successes of the French revolutionary army. From a French word for a kind of clothing much worn during the Revolution.

carphology [kar-**fah**-luh-jee] the movements of delirious patients, especially pulling at sheets or blankets, or movements that seem to suggest a search for imaginary objects. This word comes from a Greek word meaning 'collecting straw.'

carriwitchet [ka-ri-**wich**-it] a pun, a conundrum. The etymology is unknown, making the origin of the word itself a conundrum.

catoblephon [kat-uh-**bleff**-un] an unidentified African mammal described in the works of the ancients. Possibly a buffalo or a gnu, it was 'a creature like a bull, whose eyes are so fixed as chiefly to look downward.'

catoptric [kuh-**tahp**-trik] an adjective meaning 'relating to a mirror or to optical reflection.' This word comes from Greek roots meaning 'against' and 'see.'

catoptromancy [kuh-**tahp**-truh-man-see] divination, i.e., foretelling the future, by means of a mirror. The ending -*mancy* comes from a Greek word meaning 'divination': it is found in many English words for different methods of foretelling the future, for example, *scapulimancy*, divination from the cracks in a burned animal's shoulder blade, *oneiromancy*, divination from dreams, and *chiromancy*, divination from the lines on one's hands.

centessence [sen-**tess**-uhns] a nonce-word meaning 'the hundredth essence,' used in contrast to *quintessence*, which literally means 'the fifth essence.' The heavenly bodies were supposed to be made up of quintessence, and the alchemists busied themselves with trying to distill it (when they weren't busy trying to make lead into gold). The *OED* pedantically remarks that the proper word to be the analogue of *quintessence* would be *centesimessence*. We'll get right on that.

chairoplane [**chair**-uh-plane] a merry-go-round or carousel where the seats are suspended from chains, and the riders are swung outward in a circle as the center support goes around. Unfortunately, two of the citations in the *OED* have this word collocated with 'victim' and 'tragedy.' From *chair* plus the *plane* of *airplane*.

chamade [shuh-**mahd**] a signal inviting someone to a parley (usually a drumbeat or trumpet sounding). Now perhaps useful to those who have to carry beepers. "Sorry, have to go, it's a chamade."

chaston [**chas**-tun] the part of a ring that holds a stone (also called a *collet*).

chelidonize [ke-**lye**-dun-ize] to twitter like swallows, or to sing the "swallow song" of Rhodes, which was a kind of trick-or-treating activity where boys, after seeing the first swallows arrive, would go around in bands singing for food 'for the swallow.' In more recent times it has been performed on March 1st by boys carrying a wooden swallow on a pole.

chessom [**chess**-um] an adjective, usually used about soil, meaning 'without stones or grit.' No reason, though, why it couldn't be used for oysters and spinach.

chiliad [**kill**-ee-ad] a group of a thousand things, especially a period of a thousand years. (Since I discovered this word much too late to be of any use for the last turn-of-the-millennium, I have grandiose, Walt Disneyesque plans for making sure I have an opportunity to use it next time . . .)

chirocracy [kye-**rah**-kruh-see] a very rare word meaning 'government by physical force.'

chiurm [**chee**-urm] an obsolete word for a group of galley slaves; also used contemptuously for any gang. This word seems suited to abuse by bad middle managers or use by hard-boiled police officers.

choical [**koy**-i-cle] a Gnostic term, coming from a Greek word for 'dust.' The Gnostics believed that the visible body was made up of two parts: a "subtle element" that they called the *hylic body*, and a "sheath of gross earthly matter" that they called the *choical body*.

choil [choil] the name of the indented part of a pocketknife where the edge of the blade adjoins the tang or thick part by which it is hafted, or the corresponding part of any knife where the cutting edge ends. To *choil* is to make this indention or slope in a knife, and a *choiler* is an instrument for making the *choil*. The *OED* says, "*Choil* has been used in Sheffield from before the memory of the oldest inhabitant."

choller [**chah**-ler] a double chin, or the hanging lip of a hound dog.

choronymy [ko-**rah**-nuh-mee] the study of naming, especially place names and names for geographical phenomena, including wind names, hurricane names, and astronomical names. The roots *choro*- and -*nymy* come from the Greek words for 'place' and 'name.'

circumvallate [ser-kuhm-**va**-late] a literary verb meaning 'to surround with a rampart or wall.' The word originated in the seventeenth century as an adjective based on Latin words meaning 'around' and 'rampart.' As an adjective, it does in fact have a special anatomical sense in modern English: it refers to small rounded protuberances, or *papillae*, near the back of the tongue, that are surrounded by taste receptors.

claick [klayk] the last armful of grain cut at harvest, also called the *kirn-cut, maiden*, or *kirn-baby*. It was often kept and hung by a ribbon above the fireplace.

clavus [**klay**-vuhs] a pain in the forehead, as though a nail were being driven into it, associated with hysteria. This word comes from a Latin word meaning 'nail.'

clivose [**klye**-vohs] an adjective meaning 'hilly, steep.' It comes from the Latin word *clivosus*, which has the same meaning.

cockagrice [**kahk**-uh-grice] an unappetizing (to modern palates) dish made of an old cock and a pig boiled and roasted together. *Grice* is an old word for pig.

cockyolly bird [kahk-ee-**ahl**-ee] an expression meaning 'dear little bird,' used both about birds and as an endearment. It is a variant of *dicky-bird*.

codology [kahd-**ah**-luh-jee] an Irish word meaning, jocularly, 'the science of leg-pulling.' *Cod* is an Irishism for a joke or a hoax. A hoaxer is called a *codologist*.

colliby [**kall**-ih-bee] a little present. Most likely from a Greek word meaning 'small coin' or 'small cake'—both useful small presents for children.

colophonian [kah-luh-**foh**-nee-uhn] a spurious word, meaning 'relating to a colophon or the conclusion of a book,' originally a mistake for *Colophonian* (with a capital *C*), which means 'an inhabitant of Colophon.' However, the word could still be redeemed—there isn't a word now that means 'relating to a colophon, etc.' (even though there is the word *colophonize*, meaning 'to give a book a colophon'), and this word is as good a candidate as any. *Colophon* (the book word, meaning the inscription at the end of a book that gives facts about its publication, design, etc., or a publisher's emblem on the spine or title page) ultimately comes from a Greek word meaning 'summit, finishing touch.'

comminatory [**kah**-min-uh-to-ree] or [kuh-**min**-uh-to-ree] a rare word meaning 'threatening, punitive, or vengeful.' It is related to *commination*, which means 'the threatening of divine vengeance'; both words come from a Latin verb meaning 'to threaten.' In the Anglican liturgy, *commination* refers to the recital of divine threats against sinners that forms part of the service for Ash Wednesday.

contango [kuhn-**tang**-go] in the pre-computer age, the fee that a buyer of stock pays to the seller to postpone transfer of the stock to the next or any future settlement date. It was usually paid on a per share or percent basis. The word also has a modern meaning, 'the condition in which distant delivery prices for futures exceed spot prices, often due to the costs of storing and insuring the commodity.' The antonym of *contango* is *backwardation*.

concinnous [kun-**sin**-us] a neat and elegant adjective meaning 'neat, elegant.'

consuetudinary [kahns-wi-**t(y)oo**-duh-ner-ee] a guide to customs, rituals, or practices, especially those of a religious order.

corrade [kuh-**rade**] an obsolete word meaning 'to gather together from various sources.' From a Latin word meaning 'to scrape together.' One of the early citations (1619) from the *OED* makes the excuse of anthologists everywhere: "I haue made choise of mine Authors, not *corrading* out of all promiscue."

coshering [**kahsh**-er-ing] an obsolete and rare Irish word meaning 'feasting.' Also, the tradition among Irish chiefs of paying extended (and most likely expensive) visits to their dependents or tenants. A 1612 citation in the *OED* remarks that "the lord . . . did eat them out of house and home." The noun is *coshery*.

cosmothetic [kahz-moh-**thet**-ik] an adjective meaning 'something that assumes there is an external world.' It is used about a theory of perception that posits the existence of an external world but denies that we have any evidence of it or knowledge about it. Perhaps useful for describing such statements such as "I know there are people who put mayonnaise on hot dogs, but I've never met one myself." From Greek words meaning 'world' plus 'positing.'

couthie [**koo**-thee] a Scottish word, used to describe a person as 'warm and friendly' or a place as 'cosy and comfortable.' The word arose in the early eighteenth century, apparently from Old English *cuth*, meaning 'known.'

crapulous [**krap**-yoo-luhs] a literary word meaning 'relating to drunkenness or the drinking of alcohol.' Like the related adjective *crapulent* and noun *crapulence*, it comes from a Latin word meaning 'inebriation,' itself based on a Greek word meaning 'drunken headache.'

cremett [**krem**-it] another spurious word, this one a mistaken reading of *eremite*, meaning 'inmate of a hospital.' *Eremite* can also mean 'hermit.' One can make a nice, completely wrong folk etymology for the mistake by concluding that since people saw hermits so infrequently, of course they couldn't keep the word straight.

crimp [krimp] someone who tricks sailors and soldiers into service, especially by decoying or impressing them.

criticaster [kri-ti-**kas**-ter] a minor or incompetent critic. The ending *-aster* is used to form nouns referring to someone who is inept or unskillful in a certain sphere of activity, for example, *poetaster*, a person who writes bad poetry, or *medicaster*, a person who falsely claims to have medical skill.

cromulent [**krahm**-yoo-luhnt] an adjective meaning 'acceptable; legitimate.' This word comes from an episode of *The Simpsons* in which Bart's teacher, Miss Krabappel, remarks, "*Embiggens*? I never heard that word before I moved to Springfield." Lisa's teacher, Miss Hoover, replies, "I don't know why. It's a perfectly *cromulent* word." In another episode, Bart makes up the word *kwyjibo*, meaning 'a big, dumb, balding North American ape. With no chin,' which he tries to use in a game of Scrabble with Homer.

croquembouche [**kro**-kum-boosh] a pyramid of pastries, usually cream-filled, covered with spun caramel. When used as a wedding cake, the bride and groom traditionally smash the hard caramel coating with a hammer. From a French word that means 'crunches in the mouth.'

cruentation [kroo-en-**tay**-shun] the term for the oozing of blood which occasionally occurs when a cut is made into a dead body. Formerly it was used to mean the supposed bleeding from wounds that would happen when the body of a murdered person was in the presence of the murderer. This comes from a Latin word meaning 'staining with blood.'

crumenically [kroo-**mee**-nick-lee] an adverb meaning 'relating to the purse.' One of many coinages by Samuel Taylor Coleridge (1772–1834), who obviously had quite a bit of time on his hands, and often financial worries on his mind.

cryptaesthesia [krip-tiss-**thee**-zhuh] any kind of supernormal perception, including clairvoyance and telepathy. From *crypto-* and a Greek word meaning 'perception.'

cuadrilla [kwah-**drill**-yuh] the troupe belonging to a matador, including his picadors, banderilleros, and a cachetero.

cultrivorous [kul-**triv**-er-us] a rare adjective meaning 'swallowing (or pretending to swallow) knives.' From Latin words meaning 'knife' and 'to devour.'

cul-de-lampe [**kyool**-duh-lahmp] an ornament or little drawing used to fill up white space on a printed page. From a French word meaning 'lamp-bottom,' as the shape of the ornament was reminiscent of the bottom of an ancient lamp.

cumber-ground [**kum**-ber-ground] a person who needlessly takes up space, especially someone who is useless in his or her job.

cunctipotent [kungk-**tip**-uh-tunt] an ill-sounding synonym for *omnipotent*, with the same meaning. *Cunctitenent* means 'having all things.'

cuniculous [kyoo-**nick**-yuh-lus] an obsolete adjective meaning 'full of rabbits.' Suitable for stereotypical magicians everywhere. From a Latin word meaning 'abounding in caves.'

CUMBER-GROUND

He can't talk right now - I'm on the phone

curculionideous [kur-kyoo-lee-uh-**nid**-ee-dus] an adjective meaning 'pertaining to weevils.' Now you can say, "Please don't tell me that *curculionideous* pun again!"

curwhibble [kur-**whib**-ble] a thingamajig, a whatchamacallit.

cymbocephalic [sim-boh-suh-**fal**-ick] having a skull shaped like a boat, especially when seen from above; having a long and narrow skull. From Greek words meaning 'boat' and 'head.'

43

dabbity [**dab**-bit-ee] a Scottish word for little ornaments or decorations for a mantelpiece, especially china animals, souvenirs, etc.

dactylioglyph [dack-**till**-ee-uh-gliff] an engraver of (finger) rings or the inscription of the name of the engraver or artist on a ring or gem. *Dactyliology* is the study of finger rings, and *dactyliomancy* is the art of telling the future by means of finger rings.

dactylonomy [dack-tuh-**lah**-nuh-mee] the science of counting on your fingers. A nice saving term for people who are bad at math. "I'm a *dactylonomist*, actually. It's very difficult to be a good one." *Chisanbop* is a Korean method of using the fingers as an abacus; on the left hand each finger is counted as ten and the thumb as fifty and on the right hand the thumb is five and the fingers each one. So counting 22 would involve pressing down the first two fingers on the left hand and the first two of the right; adding the thumb of the left and the remaining two fingers of the right add 52; then you can read the total, 74, from your pressed-down fingers. *Chisanbop* comes from Korean words meaning 'finger counting method.'

darraign [der-**rain**] to prepare someone to fight, to fit someone out for battle. Also, to decide something by combat (other than who's the best fighter). This word comes from an Old French word meaning 'to explain, defend.'

DEPRESSING AND DISPIRITING DEATH WORDS

Death may not be pleasant to contemplate, but the words dealing with death often are. Whether you're a *crack-halter* (likely to die on the gallows) or actually *patibulate* (sentenced to death by hanging), whether you commit *junshi* (suicide upon the death of your lord) or are stricken with *kwashiorkor* (a wasting disease caused by lack of protein), whether you believe in *excarnation* (the separation of the soul from the body at death) or *psychopannychy* (the sleep of the soul between death and the day of judgment), death comes for us all.

One would hope, however, that our *stour* (conflict with death) is easy, and without an offputting *ruckle* (death-rattle), and that we are not the recipient of a *letter to Uriah* (a letter that pretends to be friendly but is in fact a death-warrant). It seems preferable to die in a *holmgang* (duel to the death) than to have someone *jugulate* (kill by cutting the throat) you. And certainly hearing shouts of "*Crucifige!*" ('crucify!') would be unpleasant.

It would be good to have some kind of warning: maybe to *hear the Alpleich* (music heard before death) or *see a fetch-light* (a spectral light traveling from the house of a person about to die to his or her grave) or perhaps to hear the cry of the *lich-owl* (which supposedly portends death in the house), or to see a *wag-at-the-wall* (a ghost that haunts the kitchen and moves backwards and forwards before the death of one of the family) just to get your affairs in order, of course. Or perhaps your horoscope showed an *anareta* (the killing planet, threatening death) or an *interfector* (a death-bringing planet)? Even if it gave you fair warning, a visit from a *barghest* (a goblin in the form of a large and horrible dog, foretelling death or misfortune) would be unsettling. Once you are warned and have possibly received extreme unction, you might want to follow *endura*, a practice of the Cathari, where those who have received spiritual baptism endure physical privations that often result in death, to avoid recontamination of their souls. Of course, at death, it was formerly believed, your *eye-strings* (the muscles, tendons, or nerves of the eye) break. If you share your death with another person (both in the same accident, or at the same astrological time, but separated) you can be called *commorient*.

Once you're dead, certain proprieties must be observed—you shouldn't be *lying by the wall* (dead but not buried), and your family should give the clergy a *corse-present* (a customary gift at death and burial) from your remaining chattels, if the priest hasn't already claimed the *umest* (the coverlet of a bed, often claimed by a priest at the death of a parishioner). It is to be hoped that those chattels don't include *Nachlass* (writings unpublished at the author's death). If you were in a *tontine* (a scheme by which the members of a common fund each receive a regular payment during their lives, which goes up as other members die, until the last member receives the whole amount), your *co-tontineurs* may not be overwhelmed by grief at your passing.

If by chance you were killed abroad, your fellow-citizens at home could decide to practice *androlepsy*, where, according to Athenian law, they could seize three subjects of the offending country in reprisal. Although if your death were a *sparagmos* (in mythology, the tearing apart or other ritual death of a hero as part of a cycle of death and rebirth) you might just want them to hold off and wait for the cycle to begin again. At least you weren't subject to *Jedwood justice*, being put to death first and put on trial afterwards.

deasil [**dee**-zuhl]   an adverb meaning 'clockwise' or 'in the direction of the sun's course,' a direction considered by some to bring luck or good fortune. It comes from a Scottish Gaelic word and is rarely used today; its opposite, *widdershins*, meaning 'anticlockwise' or 'in the opposite direction to the sun's course,' is much less rare.

decemnovenarianize [di-sem-no-vi-**na**-ree-uh-nize]   to act like a person of the nineteenth century (a *decemnovenarian*).

decussate [**deh**-kuh-sate] or [di-**kuss**-ate]   having the form of an *X*. This comes from a Latin word meaning 'the number ten' (the Roman numeral for which is, of course, X).

deesis [dee-**ee**-sis]   an invocation of, or address to, a supreme being.

defluvium [duh-**floo**-vee-uhm]   the shedding of some body part because of disease. Before you picture people dropping arms, legs, and ears left and right, let me reassure you that the parts lost are usually hair and fingernails.

deglutition [dee-gloo-**tish**-uhn]   the action of swallowing. The verb, even rarer than the noun, is *deglute*. It could be brought back into fashion with a new figurative sense: "You can't expect me to *deglute* that excuse! What a feat of *deglutition* that would be."

deipnosophist [dype-**nah**-suh-fist]   a master of the art of dining. This comes from a Greek word meaning 'one learned in the mysteries of the kitchen.' The plural of this word in Greek was the title of a work by Athenaeus, in which erudite men discuss not only the dishes they were eating but also literary criticism and other miscellaneous topics.

dejerate [**dedj**-uh-rate] an obsolete word meaning 'to take an oath, to swear to something.'

delassation [dee-lass-**say**-shun] fatigue, tiredness. Even saying *delassation* makes you tired. From a Latin word meaning 'to tire out.'

deliciate [di-**lish**-ee-ate] an unfortunately obsolete word meaning 'to make yourself happy; to indulge; to revel.' Perhaps through *abligurition?*

delitescent [dell-i-**tess**-unt] an adjective meaning 'hidden, concealed.'

deodand [**dee**-o-dand] an object that has been the direct cause of the death of a human being (such as a boat from which a person has fallen and drowned) and has been given to the King to be used as an offering to God. This word comes from the Latin for 'that is to be given to God.' This custom was abolished in England in 1846.

desticate [**des**-ti-kate] a deservedly rare and obsolete word that means 'to squeak like a rat.' Perhaps due, though, for a new life in mobster shows. The noun *destication*, 'squeaking,' isn't much more common.

deturpate [**dee**-tur-pate] an ugly word with an ugly meaning: 'to disfigure, to defile.' From Latin words meaning 'to make ugly.'

deuterogamist [d(y)oo-ter-**rah**-guh-mist] someone who marries a second time. Or, as the old joke goes, an optimist.

diazingiber [dye-uh-**zin**-ji-ber] a kind of ginger candy. *Dia-* is a Greek root meaning 'made of.'

dictioneer [dic-shun-**eer**] a slighting term for people who take it upon themselves to criticize diction or writing style. *Dictioneers* are very rarely invited to comment, but that never stops them!

dignotion [dig-**noh**-shun] a distinguishing mark or sign. This seems to have a mainly abstract use, instead of being a quick way to say "any birthmarks, tattoos, scars, or brandings?" From a Latin word meaning 'to distinguish.'

dilluing [dill-**loo**-ing] the process of sorting ore by washing it in a hand sieve. Also written *deluing*. It would be surprising if any of the prospectors of 1848, or any other gold rush, knew this word for their activity.

dimidiate [di-**mid**-ee-ate] to divide into half or reduce by half. Something that is divided in half can be called *dimidiate*, as can a hermaphrodite.

disboscation [dis-bahs-**kay**-shuhn] the clearing of woods to make farmland or pasture. This word isn't used today but could be revived in protests against the clearing of woodland for more shopping malls or housing developments.

disidemony [diz-eh-duh-**mohn**-ee] an obsolete word meaning worshipping a god or gods from fear, and not from love. From a Greek word meaning 'fear of the gods'

discerp [dis-**surp**] to tear something to shreds, to tear something apart, to separate. From a Latin word meaning 'pluck.'

disembogue [dis-em-**bohg**] used of a river or stream, this verb means 'to emerge or pour out.' It is found mainly in literary writing and comes from a Spanish word meaning 'to come out of the mouth of a river.'

douzepers [dooz-**perrz**] a plural noun, being the twelve paladins of Charlemagne, who were the bravest of his knights. The word can also be used to refer to other illustrious knights or nobles.

Dowsabel [**dows**-uh-bel] a form of the name *Dulcibella*, used to mean 'sweetheart.'

draffsack [**draf**-sak] a bag of garbage, used figuratively to mean 'a big paunch or belly, a glutton.' *Draff* is an old word meaning 'dregs, swill.'

dragoman [**drag**-uh-muhn] an interpreter or professional guide for travelers, especially one in countries in which Arabic, Turkish, or Persian is spoken. It comes from an Arabic word meaning 'interpreter.'

drail [drale] an obsolete word meaning 'a long trailing headdress.' However, the vagaries of fashion being what they are, who knows if it will remain obsolete?

Draisine [dray-**zeen**] the earliest kind of bicycle, named after its inventor, Baron von Drais of Sauerbrun. He called it a *swiftwalker* (he was a modest fellow, it seems). It was also called a *dandy-horse*.

Drawcansir [draw-**kan**-ser] someone who kills or injures both friend and foe. From the name of a blustering, bragging character in George Villiers's burlesque play *The Rehearsal*, who in the last scene is made to enter a battle and to kill all the combatants on both sides. His name might be intended to suggest drawing a can of liquor, as there are references to his drinking capacity in the fourth act of the play.

drazel [**drazz**-zle] a slut. Of unknown origin, perhaps connected with the Scots word *drasie*, which may or may not mean 'phlegmatic.'

dretch [drech] an obsolete word meaning both 'to trouble in sleep' and 'to be troubled in sleep.' It's from an Old English word and is unknown in other Germanic languages, although we know that everyone has bad dreams, at least occasionally. A citation from Malory's *Le Morte d'Arthur* reads "We alle ... were soo dretched that somme of vs lepte oute of oure beddes naked," which must be the canonical bad awakening.

drinkdom [**dringk**-dum] the influence of the alcoholic beverage industry, or the power of drink. The *OED* gives an 1885 citation, "The triumph of *drinkdom* over temperance."

drogulus [**drah**-gyuh-lus] something the presence of which cannot be verified, usually a disembodied being, because it has no physical effects. Coined by the philosopher A. J. Ayer, possibly by association with *dragon*.

dromaeognathous [drah-mee-**agg**-nuh-thus] having a palate like than of an emu. This is such a wonderful word that it's a shame that most people would have to work extremely hard to wangle this into conversation. In fact, it may be impossible.

drong [drahng] a narrow lane or alley. From an Old English word meaning 'to press, to compress.'

drumble [**drum**-ble] to move in a slow or sluggish way, to be lazy. Also, to drone or mumble.

druxy [**druck**-see] an adjective meaning 'having rotten spots concealed by healthy wood.' A nice candidate for extension—how many rotten things are concealed by seemingly sound exteriors?

dulocracy [doo-**lah**-kruh-see] government by slaves. Used mostly in the sense of "heaven forbid these inferior people ever rule us," instead of "finally the enslaved get their turn and rightful place." This word doesn't seem have been used much even in the heated antebellum era, when you would have thought it would get a workout.

dulosis [d(y)oo-**loh**-sis] the technical term for the enslavement of ants, by ants. The adjective is *dulotic*. Sadly, there has never been an ant Abraham Lincoln, so there is no ant Emancipation Proclamation, or even any ant Harriet Beecher Stowe.

dyslogistic [dis-luh-**djiss**-tick] expressing disapproval or opprobrium. The antonym of *eulogistic*.

dysteleology [dis-tell-ee-**ah**-luh-djee] the study of the organs of plants and animals without admitting that there is any purpose to their design. The antonym is *teleology*, studying things with the idea that there is a purpose for everything in nature. Someone who is unwilling to admit the existence of design in nature has *teleophobia*.

ECHOPRAXIA

eadness [**ed**-niss] an obsolete word meaning 'happiness, luxury.' From an Old English word meaning 'wealth.' It seems that the idea of money buying happiness is very old in English—this word has a citation from the year 1000.

eagre [**ee**-guhr] a wave of unusual height, especially a tidal wave up a narrow estuary. The origin remains unknown.

eblandish [ee-**blan**-dish] an obsolete and rare word meaning 'to get by coaxing or flattery,' from a Latin word with the same meaning.

eboulement [ay-**bool**-munt] the crumbling or falling of a wall, especially a fortification. This is another good word demanding figurative use. "She's still hanging up when I call, but I'm hoping for an *eboulement* soon."

eccaleobion [eck-kal-ee-oh-**bye**-un] the name given to an egg-hatching machine invented in 1839 by a W. Bucknell. The name is supposed to be the sentence "I evoke life" written as one Greek word. It has been used figuratively; a citation from 1880 in the *OED* says that a particular magazine was "at one time a very *eccaleöbion* for young writers."

echopraxia [eck-oh-**prack**-see-uh] the meaningless imitation of the movements of others, probably including that parlor trick where you yawn or scratch your nose and watch the movement make its way through all the people in a room. From *echo* and the Greek word for 'action.'

ecopoiesis [ee-ko-**po**-ee-sis] a word invented by Robert Haynes, a Canadian scientist. *Ecopoeisis* is the creation of an ecosystem on a barren planet. He derived it from Greek words meaning 'house' and 'creation.'

elaqueate [e-**lack**-we-ate] to free from a noose or other entanglement. Another literal word that needs a figurative sense: "At first, I felt bad about being laid off, but then I realized I'd been *elaqueated*." A related rare word is *illaqueable*, meaning 'capable of being snared': "I applied there, but I realized the job I wanted wasn't *illaqueable*."

emacity [e-**may**-si-tee] a fondness for buying things. The word comes from a Latin verb meaning 'to buy': it has always been extremely rare and, despite the increasing materialism of recent decades, shows no sign of becoming any less so!

emmetropia [em-uh-**troh**-pee-uh] the condition of the eye in which no correction of vision is needed—in other words, 20/20 vision or better. From Greek words meaning '(well) proportioned' and 'eye.' If both eyes have the same vision, they are *isometropic*.

empasm [em-**paz**-'m] a perfumed powder sprinkled on the body to prevent sweating or for medicinal purposes. A similar word with the same meaning is *diapasm*: both come from a Greek verb meaning 'to sprinkle.' There is no recorded use of either word since the late nineteenth century.

emulous [**em**-yuh-lus] an adjective meaning 'wanting to rival or imitate, wanting to obtain.' It also means 'motivated by rivalry' or 'greedy for praise or power.' This last meaning is a reasonable extension, for who is *emulous* of someone weak or despised? This word is a nice way to say *envious, jealous,* and *emulative,* all at once.

emunctory [e-**munk**-tuh-ree] relating to the blowing of the nose. Emunction is 'the action of wiping the nose.' Both these words come from Latin words with the same meanings. The rare word *emunct,* meaning 'of keen or acute judgment,' comes from a Latin phrase that means 'a man of keen scent' or 'a man with a wiped nose.'

emydosaurian [e-mi-do-**saw**-ree-uhn] a crocodile. This fancy term comes from the roots *emyd-,* meaning 'turtle,' and -*saurian,* meaning 'lizard.'

encarpa [en-**kar**-puh] an obsolete and rare word for architectural decorations featuring fruit. From a Greek word meaning 'containing fruit.'

enchorial [en-**kor**-ee-ul] an adjective meaning 'used in or belonging to a particular country.' It comes from a Greek word meaning 'in or of the country.' An 1882 citation from the *OED* reads "That indescribable *enchorial* something which is British and not Netherlandish."

entermete [en-tur-**meet**] an obsolete word meaning 'to meddle, to concern oneself (with something),' the implication being of course "something that is none of your business." From two Latin forms, one meaning 'to interrupt,' the other meaning 'to send.'

entortillation [en-tor-ti-**lay**-shuhn] the action of entwining or twisting. This comes from a Latin word meaning 'to twist.'

epagomenic [ep-uh-**gah**-muh-nick] denoting days left off the calendar (before calendar reform). Also, gods worshiped on those days. This would be a lovely word to use for holidays that are personal but not public; birthdays, anniversaries, mental health days, and the like. "I need next Tuesday off, it's an *epagomenic* day."

ephorize [**ef**-uh-rize] to rule, to have a controlling influence on. From the title given to magistrates in various Dorian states, especially Sparta, where the five *ephors*, appointed annually by popular election, exercised a controlling power over the kings. From a Greek word meaning 'overseer.'

epinicion [ep-ee-**nee**-see-un] a song sung in honor of the winner of the games, or a song of triumph. A very fancy term for anything played over a stadium's PA system. From Greek words meaning 'upon' and 'victory.'

epirot [ip-**pye**-rut] a person who lives inland, not on the coast. From a Greek word meaning 'mainland.' A word that those of us in "flyover country" can use with pride.

epithymy [i-**pith**-uh-mee] a rare word meaning 'desire, lust.' The term is obsolete, but the adjective of choice that pairs with this idea hasn't changed since 1600: the *OED* citation has "hot *epithymie.*"

equivoque [**eck**-wuh-voke] something that has the same name as something else, such as the six Sarahs in your child's class at school.

erethism [**err**-i-thiz-'m] painful, unhealthy overexcitement, especially of the mental powers or passions. This comes from a Greek word meaning 'to irritate,' and a misspelling, *erythism*, appeared in quite a few medical books.

ergophobic [er-guh-**foh**-bik] someone who fears work. Usually, this word is used jocularly.

erinaceous [err-i-**nay**-shuhs] an adjective meaning 'like a hedgehog.' It is mostly used in a zoological sense but cries out for a figurative use to describe people with prickly or bristly manners.

erubescent [err-oo-**bess**-uhnt] a rare adjective meaning 'reddening or blushing.' It is based on a Latin verb meaning 'to be red': a related word in English is *rubicund*, an adjective which refers to a ruddy or high-colored facial complexion.

esemplastic [es-em-**plas**-tik] an adjective meaning 'molding into one' or 'unifying.' Coined by Samuel Taylor Coleridge (1772–1834) in the early nineteenth century to refer to the power of the human imagination, it was probably suggested by a German word with the same meaning, *Ineinsbildung*. There are very few recorded examples of its use outside Coleridge's own writings.

etaoin shrdlu [**ett**-oh-in **shurd**-loo] the letters set by hitting the first two vertical banks of keys on the left side of the keyboard of a Linotype machine. This sequence is used as a temporary placeholder but is also sometimes printed by mistake. *Etaoin shrdlu* is also used to mean any error-filled sequence of type.

ethnophaulism [eth-no-**fall**-izm] an ethnic slur, or an expression (such as *Dutch courage,* meaning 'bravery induced by alcoholic drink') containing a disparaging allusion to another group. (While we're disparaging the Dutch, *Flounderkin* is an obsolete ethnophaulism for a Dutchman.) This is also called an *achthronym.* From a Greek word meaning 'to hold cheap.'

eustress [**yoo**-stress] good stress, such as a promotion or a new baby. It makes you happy, it makes you crazy, but with a little more happy than crazy. From Greek *eu-* ('good') and *stress.*

eutrapely [yoo-**trap**-uh-lee] a sadly obsolete word for 'pleasantness in conversation,' one of the seven moral virtues enumerated by Aristotle. In the New Testament, it was used to mean 'a reprehensible levity of speech.'

exauctorate [eks-**awk**-tuh-rate] to depose or oust from office, to deprive of authority. This comes from a Latin word meaning 'to dismiss from service.'

exonym [**eks**-o-nim] a name that foreigners use for a place (instead of the name that people who live there use), such as *Cologne* for *Köln* and *Florence* for *Firenze.*

expergefaction [eks-per-ji-**fak**-shuhn] waking up, from a Latin word meaning 'make awake.' Alarm clocks could be called *expergefactors.*

EXTRAORDINARY AND
EXCITING EXCLAMATIONS

Although we can be sure that human emotions haven't changed much, if at all, during the past several millennia, the words we use to show those emotions—or to add stress or emphasis or agreement—certainly have.

Not very many people have used *adad!* since the late 1700s, no matter how strongly they feel the need to emphasize their feelings. (The last citation in the *OED* is "Why you look as fresh and bloomy to-day—Adad, you little slut, I believe you are painted" from 1763.) Likewise, *avoy!* as 'an expression of fear, surprise, or remonstrance' hasn't seen much use either. (The last citation, from 1393, being "Avoy my lorde, I am a maide.") *Coads-nigs!*, an expression of surprise, would be itself surprising to hear today.

Many a light oath of the last couple of centuries, however relieving to the feelings of those who once said them, are opaque today. *Ifegs!*, *ifads!*, *ivads!*, *mafey!*, and *fegs!*, all expressing astonishment and all related to *faith*, would be usefully resurrected by those wanting that hard-to-achieve swashbuckling air. Even more swashbuckling and devil-may-care is *jernie!*, an oath meaning 'I renounce God' (originally from the French *je renie Dieu*). *'Sdines* ('by God's *dines*', or 'dignity') lacks strength as an oath, but you have to admire the invention of *'Slidikins!* ('by God's eyelids'). Exclaiming *'Snails!* might cause people to look for slimy little shelled creatures and wonder about your phobic tendencies; nobody would think that you were swearing 'by God's nails.'

Fludgs! meaning 'quickly' is wasted in a dusty corner of the dictionary: *Fludgs!*—bring it back! *Gip!* and *gup!*, used to express irritation to a horse, don't seem to be that useful today, unless people want non-digital ways to express their impatience with other drivers. *Hissa!*, used by seamen when hauling or hoisting, doesn't translate well to the metaphorical heavy lifting many of us do during the workday. And *hyke!* or *stoo!*, used to call dogs to the chase, won't do so much for motivating the football team. *Sess!*, used to call a dog to dinner, though, could be picked up again by dogs fairly quickly. Cats may still have to listen for the can opener.

Ichane!, an expression of sorrow (possibly from a Gaelic word meaning 'oh, alas'), still sounds suitably sad and lonesome; *tilly-vally!*, meaning 'nonsense', is likewise still perfectly clear, but *lew!* meaning 'behold' is now just silly. *Proface!* as an expression of good wishes at dinner (from a French phrase meaning 'may it do you good') would be a nice way to start a meal. *Tphrowh!*, used to draw attention, would be useful if only I had a clue as to how to pronounce it. (I'm sure all my efforts at doing so would draw attention, if not the kind I was hoping for.) It's also hard to believe that *wahahowe!* ever served anybody well as an expression of surprise; it looks more like a transliteration of a sneeze. *Zoonters!*, on the other hand, could come out of the mouth of any fourteen-year-old on the planet: *"Zoonters* they're gone" is the citation in the *OED*. Well, *zoonters!* These words may be gone for now, but it doesn't mean they can't come back.

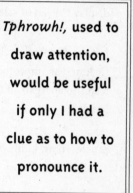

Tphrowh!, **used to draw attention, would be useful if only I had a clue as to how to pronounce it.**

factice [fak-**tees**] a perfume bottle, usually hugely oversized, made for display instead of sale.

faitour [**fay**-ter] a cheat, especially a person who shams illness or tells fortunes; an impostor. Since there never seem to be enough derogatory terms to apply to all those who deserve them, this word may come in handy.

fankle [**fang**-kuhl] a Scottish word meaning 'to tangle or entangle something.' It comes from Scots *fank*, which means 'a coil of rope.'

farandman [fuh-**rand**-man] an obsolete Scottish law term for a stranger or traveler. The *law of farandman* allowed for a pedlar who didn't reside in a jurisdiction to bring someone up on charges of theft, and required that the trial should happen before the tide had gone in and out three times.

feminisma [fem-in-**eez**-muh] a word used by the novelist Agnes Rossi, formed on the model of *machismo,* to describe the quality and display of feminine pride, especially based on childbearing and child-rearing.

Fescennine [**fes**-suh-neen] an obscene or insulting song or verses. From a Latin term for Fescennia in Etruria, which was famous for insulting verses.

festuceous [fes-**too**-shuhs] an obsolete and rare word meaning 'like a straw.' A related word is *festucaceous*, which means 'like a stalk.' They both come from a Latin root meaning 'stalk.'

feuillemorte [fuhy-**mort**] an adjective meaning 'having the color of a dead or faded leaf' (i.e., brown or yellowish brown). It comes from the French for 'dead leaf.' Other, less Frenchy forms are *filemot, philemort,* and *phillimot.*

fiant [**fee**-unt] an obsolete word meaning '(of an animal, especially badgers and foxes) to cast excrement.'

finifugal [fye-**nif**-yoo-gul] an adjective meaning 'shunning the end (of anything).' Appropriate both for children avoiding bedtime and for those folks who "just don't want the book to end."

finnesko [**fins**-koh] a boot made of reindeer skin tanned with birch, with the hair left on the outside. A fashion statement made on early polar expeditions and trips across Greenland.

finnimbrun [fin-**nim**-brun] a knickknack, a trinket.

fiscelle [fis-**sell**] a little basket. Probably one of those baskets which somehow seem to persist, filled with paper clips and unrecognizable parts of unremembered objects, long after the original contents have vanished.

fistiana [fis-tee-**ann**-uh] a humorous word meaning 'of or relating to the fists or boxing.' Synonyms are *fistic* and *fistical;* the *OED* haughtily remarks that these words 'are not in dignified use.'

fittyland [**fit**-ee-land] the near horse of the rearmost pair hitched to a plow, which walks on the unplowed part while the far horse walks in the furrow.

FLAFFER

Your damn flaffering kept me up all night!

flaffer [**flaff**-er] to rustle when moving, to flutter. The citations in the
OED seem to show that this word was used mostly about birds, but it
seems like a useful word for impractical dresses.

flagitation [fla-ji-**tay**-shuhn] the action of asking or demanding with passion; begging. A useful word for parents everywhere: "If you don't stop that *flagitation* right now, my answer will be no!"

flambuginous [flam-**byoo**-djuh-nus] a rare adjective meaning 'deceptive, fictitious, sham.' Related to the *flam* of *flimflam* and *flamfew*, 'a gewgaw.' *Flamfew* is related to a Latin word meaning 'a bubble, a lie.'

Flamingantism [flam-ing-**gan**-tiz-um] the policy of encouraging and furthering the use of Flemish. The implied context is "in Belgium" but it would be funnier to see *Flamingantism* everywhere.

flarf [flahrf] a word coined by poet Gary Sullivan to describe (often deliberately bad) poetry written by collaging results from Google searches, or by doing search-and-replace transformations on mundane texts.

flaskisable [flas-kuh-suh-ble] an obsolete adjective meaning 'changeable.' From an Old French word meaning 'to bend.' Used mostly about people, this is a nice substitute for *flaky*.

fleechment [**fleech**-munt] flattery, cajolery, persuasive but untruthful talk. Its origin is obscure.

fleer [flear] to laugh in a disrespectful or jeering way. A rare word found mainly in literary writing, it is probably of Scandinavian origin and is related to a Norwegian and Swedish dialect verb meaning 'to grin.'

flehmen [**flay**-mun] the raising of the head and the curling of the lip as a behavior in response to stimuli, especially sex pheromones. It seems that cats and horses do it, but not so much the traditional birds and bees (nor educated fleas). From a German word that means 'curling the lip in sexual excitement.'

flemensfirth [**flem**-unz-firth] an Old English law term for the crime of harboring a banished person. It's a corruption of an Old English term that literally means 'entertainment of fugitives,' which makes you wonder that if the fugitives aren't having a really good time, is it still a crime? What if they're only smiling politely?

flexanimous [flek-**san**-i-muhs] an adjective meaning 'having the power to influence, moving, affecting.' It comes from Latin words meaning 'bend' and 'mind.'

florisugent [flo-ri-**soo**-juhnt] an adjective meaning 'sucking honey from flowers,' used for birds and insects. It comes from Latin words meaning 'flower' and 'suck.'

flosculous [**flahs**-kyuh-lus] an adjective meaning 'like a flower' or 'flowery.' From a Latin word meaning 'little flower,' which also gives us *floscule*, 'something shaped like a little flower' or 'a flowery speech' and *flosculation*, 'speaking in a flowery way.'

forbysen [fer-**bye**-zuhn] an obsolete word meaning 'an example, a parable, a proverb, or a token.' *Bysen,* by itself, can also mean 'a shocking thing.'

FREAKISH AND
FANTASTIC FORNICATIONS

Given the amount of time that people through the ages have spent either in the activity or contemplating it (if such thinking can, in fact, be called contemplation), it's not surprising that there are so many varied words defined stodgily as 'fornication.' There's the fairly ancient *forlie*, usually used with *by* or *with*, in phrases like "and with him to be *forlayne*." Coming later are other *fornicarious* words: the more entertaining *hough-magandy* (Scots, of course), *fellowred*, *patha patha*, *scortation*, and *holoury*. If you participate in such behavior, you should be prepared to hear the *lenonian* ('belonging to a bawd') terms *apple-squire*, *bismer*, *belswagger*, *holard*, *horel*, *horeling*, *limb-lifter*, *mackerel*, *molrower*, *mutton-monger*, *putour*, *putrer*, *sheep-biter*, *smockster*, *striker* (or *stringer*), or *tweak* muttered in your direction. You might also be called a *fornicarer*, which sounds like a more emotionally involved fornicator (but isn't). If accused of *bordel* or *palliardry*, you might have to pay a *lairwite* 'a fine for fornication or adultery, especially with a bondwoman.' You might "be *meynt* in joyfulnesse," of course, or have *ymone* (or *mone* or *mene*), or go *a-mollocking* (a word coined by Stella Gibbons in the hilarious *Cold Comfort Farm*). Only women are accused of *bitchery*, *drabbery*, *putery*, or *strumpery*, as much as the other sex may participate or benefit therefrom. There's *subagitate* (depending upon the circumstances, of course), which has nothing to do with what we now think of as agitation, and even less to do with submarines. *Wifthing*, an obsolete word (from *wife* + *thing*, believe it or not), can mean 'sexual intercourse'; more romantically, it can also mean 'wedding.' If your partnership is not exclusive, or your cohabitation only temporary, you can describe it as *syndyasmian* (from a Greek word meaning 'to couple.')

If the more ordinary expressions of love are not your style, you may have to resort to more unusual words. You may have *algolagnia*, and be both masochistic and sadistic. Or you might have *kleptolagnia*, and only be aroused by theft, or *iconolagnia*, like Pygmalion, and only be moved by an image of your own making. *Urolagnia* is arousal from urination, but is fairly rare. You might be invited to a *partouse*, slang for 'orgy,' or read *fladge*, pornographic literature concentrating on flagellation. And although *pornerastic* sounds like a modern word, it was used in 1870 and means 'addicted to whoremongering.' There must be a twelve-step group for whoremongerers somewhere.

There must be a twelve-step group for whoremongerers somewhere.

A rare but helpful adjective that can describe all the words above is *syngamical*, 'pertaining to copulation.' If not a word of this entertained you, perhaps you are *anaphroditous*, 'without sexual desire.'

foudroyant [foo-**droy**-uhnt] an adjective meaning 'thundering, noisy.' This word comes from a French word meaning 'to strike with lightning.'

frapaille [fruh-**pail**] a disparaging term for camp-followers of an army. It's also obsolete, but whether that's because there are no longer so many camp-followers or because they are no longer held in such disrepute is not determined.

freck [frek] an obsolete Scottish word meaning 'to move quickly or nimbly.' *To make freck* is 'to make ready,' and *freck* can also mean 'keen for mischief, ready for trouble.' The word may come from an older word meaning 'greedy' or 'courageous.'

fremescence [fri-**mes**-unce] a rare word meaning 'an incipient roaring.' Another word useful for parents, who can swoop in with a toy or other distraction when they see an infant's *fremescence.*

frigoric [fri-**gor**-ik] an imagined, nonexistent substance supposed to be the cause of cold. It's a charming idea; as if, during winter, you could just slap on some *frigoric*-repellent like sunscreen and go out happily in your bathing suit.

fuliginous [fyoo-**lij**-i-nuhs] an adjective meaning 'sooty or dusky.' Found chiefly in the literature of the past, it comes from the Latin word for 'soot.'

fumay [**fyoo**-may] an obsolete hunting term, used to describe the action of excreting, especially by a hare. Originally from a Latin word meaning 'dung.'

FRECK

funambulist [fyoo-**nam**-byoo-list] a tightrope walker. Funambulists *funambule*, if a verb is needed. These words come from the Latin words of the same meaning (it seems as though *funambuling* is a staple of western civilization). The word can also be used figuratively to describe people who think quickly on their feet.

funestation [fyoo-nes-**tay**-shuhn] an adjective meaning 'pollution from touching a dead body.' The word *funest* means 'causing death or evil, disastrous.' Both words are related to *funeral*.

furciferous [fur-**sif**-er-us] an adjective meaning 'like a rascal.' From a Latin word meaning 'fork-bearer,' which, by analogy with the forked yoke put on the necks of criminals, also came to mean 'jailbird.'

fusby [**fuz**-bee] an obsolete term of disparagement for women. One of the citations in the *OED* (from *Punch*, in 1845) reads "A fusby woman who has indulged in the vulgar weakness of giving her children fine names." Possibly from *fubsy*, which means 'fat and squat.'

fylfot [**fil**-faht] (or *fylfot cross*) another name for the design called a *cross cramponnee*, *gammadion*, or *swastika*.

gaberlunzie [gab-er-**lun**-zee] an old Scottish word for a beggar, found frequently in Scottish literature of the early nineteenth century. It was also used to refer to a *beadsman*, who was someone paid to pray for the soul of another person. The origin of the word is unknown.

galimatias [gal-uh-**mat**-ee-us] nonsense, meaningless talk. Of unknown origin, first found in the sixteenth century.

gallinipper [**gal**-i-nip-er] a large mosquito. The etymology is unclear but the word is mainly used in the United States.

gammerstang [**gam**-er-stang] a tall, awkward woman. Related words are *gomerel*, 'fool, simpleton,' and *gamphrel*, 'blockhead.' Without the 'awkward' part, such a person could be described as *leptosomatic*, 'lean and tall.'

gangrel [**gang**-grul] a child just beginning to walk.

geason [**ghee**-zun] an adjective meaning 'rare, uncommon,' and thus also 'extraordinary, amazing.' Some of the words in this book should embody both meanings of *geason*, if we've done things right.

genizah [guh-**nee**-zuh] a repository for damaged, discarded, or heretical books. From a Hebrew word meaning 'set aside, hide.'

gegge [geg] an obsolete word of obscure origin, which seems to be an equal-opportunity term of insult for both men and women.

genyplasty [**jen**-i-plas-tee] the name for reconstructive surgery of the cheek when it has been disfigured or was congenitally defective. From Greek words meaning 'cheek' and 'molded.' Since so many body parts have figurative meanings (*hand, backbone, stomach*) this could be used with the figurative meaning of *cheek*—giving someone the ability to answer back saucily when they have either lost it or never had it in the first place.

geoponic [djee-uh-**pah**-nick] an adjective meaning 'relating to farming or agriculture,' and, like most farming words, it has an extended humorous meaning of 'rustic, countrified.' As a noun, *geoponic* means 'a book about agriculture' or 'a writer on agricultural topics.' A *geoponist* is a student of agriculture.

gilly-gaupus [gil-ee-**gaw**-pus] an awkward or foolish person. A *gawpus* is also a silly person. Other words for a silly person include *chrisom* and *dotterel*.

girouette [zhir-**wet**] a weathervane, especially used figuratively to mean someone who changes opinions as the wind blows.

glaikery [**glay**-kuh-ree] foolish or giddy conduct. *Glaik* is defined in the *OED* as 'mocking deception.'

glaistig [**glas**-tik] a Gaelic word for a beautiful fairy, usually seen at the bank of a stream. Also, a hag in the shape of a goat.

gleed [gleed] a live coal, or a beam of light. This word was used in a few equally obsolete similes, such as *as red* (or *hot* or *fierce*) *as a gleed* and *to burn* (or *glow* or *glister* or *glitter*) *as a gleed*.

gleimous [**glay**-mus] a rare word meaning 'full of phlegm or mucus.' If only the condition of being full of phlegm was as rare as this word for it. *Gleimousness* is stickiness, but if something is *engleimous* it is both slimy and venomous (a winning combination). The etymology of *gleim* itself is thankfully obscure.

gloze [glohz] a note in the margin, or a commentary or explanation in a text. This word is related to *gloss* and *glossary*, and comes from a Greek word meaning 'tongue.' To *make gloze* is a rare verb phrase meaning 'to talk smoothly or flatteringly to.'

gnap [nap] an obsolete word meaning 'to bite in a snapping way'; also, 'to criticize,' or 'to clip words when speaking.' Of onomatopoeic origin.

gnast [nast] an obsolete word meaning 'a spark; the snuff of a candle.'

gongoozler [gahn-**gooz**-ler] a person who stares at activity on a canal. This highly specific word has since been broadened to mean any kind of idler or rubbernecker.

grandgore [**gran**-gor] syphilis. Another word that sounds much nicer than what it actually means.

gricer [**grye**-ser] a train-spotter, someone who braves rainy and windy station platforms to catch a glimpse of unusual trains. An unproved etymology holds that this word comes from a humorous pronunciation of *grouse*, making the connection between the supposed resemblance of train-spotting to grouse-shooting. The verb *grice* and the noun *gricing* are back-formations from *gricer*.

GONGOOZLER

gulosity [gyoo-**lahs**-i-tee] a rare word meaning 'gluttony, greediness, voracity.' *Gulous* is another rare word with the same meaning, from the same Latin root *gula-*.

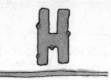

hagioscope [**hag**-ee-uh-skohp] an opening cut in the wall of a church to let worshippers in a side aisle or chapel see the elevation of the host during the service. This is also called, less graciously, a *squint*.

halch [halch] to hug or embrace. One citation for this word in the *OED*'s files, from about 1650, seems to have been used self-consciously to sound classically old-fashioned, even then.

halewey [**hal**-uh-way] an obsolete word for a kind of healing water used both internally and as a lotion. Obviously before the coining of the phrase 'for external use only.' One suspects that *halewey* was alcoholic in nature to serve such a dual purpose.

halieutic [hal-i-**yoo**-tik] an adjective meaning 'of or about fishing.' Ultimately from a Greek word meaning 'the sea.'

harbergery [**har**-ber-djuh-ree] a place of entertainment, an inn. From an Old French word meaning 'to lodge.' Grab it as the name for your restaurant now.

haslet [**hay**-slit] a piece of meat for roasting, especially the entrails of a pig or the heart or liver of a sheep or calf. From an Old French word meaning 'roasted meat.' *Hastery* is the art of roasting meat, or a collective term for roast meats. (Yet another good restaurant name.)

HASTILUDE

hastilude [**hass**-tle-ude] a kind of tournament involving spears. From Latin words meaning 'spear' and 'play.'

KEEP IT UNDER (OR ON, OR AROUND) YOUR HAT

There are probably as many interesting words for hair and hairstyles as there are hairs on your head. For instance, if you have a *peruke* (a natural head of hair) you could wear your hair in a *cadogan*, knotted behind the head, or have a *passagere*, a curled lock of hair on the temple, a *shimada*, a Japanese hairstyle of unmarried ladies, where the hair is drawn into a queue and fastened at the top of the head, or a *Newgate knocker*, a lock of hair hanging down the cheek, twisted back from the temple towards the ear. You could wear a *roach*, a roll of hair brushed up and back from the face, or perhaps (for the very brave) a *tutulus*, a Roman hairstyle where the hair is braided in a cone above the forehead.

To make these styles you might have to *frounce* (frizz) or *thrum* (curl) your hair; put it up in *papillote* (curl papers) or indulge in *pectination* (combing of the hair). You could try *piping* (wrapping the hair around clay pipes or wooden dowels), but if you are *jubate* (have a fringe of hair like a mane) or your hair is *shirl* (rough), has a *sprunt* (cowlick), or if you suffer from *plica* (a matted and dirty condition of the hair resulting from disease) you might have to visit the *poller* (barber) and resort to *rasure* (shaving your head). Seeing your shaved head might make others' hair *gresell* (stand on end) or *stiver* (bristle). If all else fails you can try a *postiche* (a piece of false hair), but I wouldn't make it the *proudfall* (front hair).

If your *trammel* (braids or tresses of hair) is suitably arranged, including the *shode* (the parting of the hair) you can move on to the next stage of your *tiff* (manner of dressing your hair) by adding a *bourgoigne* (which is only defined as 'the first part of the dress for the head next the hair'). If that's a bit too obscure, you could wear a *sévigné*, which is a kind of bandeau or ornament for the hair, or a *kell* (a hair net), from which a *wimpler* (waving lock of hair) or *plex* (braid) might escape. There's also the *tressure* (a band or filet worn around the head). If you go the tressure route and you are under a certain age, you have a *cockernony* ('the gathering of a young woman's hair, when it is wrapped up in a band or filet'). If you are not under that certain age, perhaps your hair is *lyard* (silvery gray approaching white) or you suffer from *poliosis*, premature whitening of the hair. *Piecrust hair* doesn't sound appealing (who wants a hair in their pie?) but it means having hair of a light golden brown, like piecrust.

If you were one of the original residents of Athens (before Solon's time, naturally) you could indulge in a golden *tettix* in your hair, to symbolize your status.

Once your hair is dressed and ornamented, it is time to turn your attention to your hat. If your hat is, in fact, a turban (and why not?) or a *Moab* (a kind of hat shaped like a turban) you could add a *sirpesh* (an ornament of gold, silver, or jewels worn on a turban) to it, and above that you could attach a *culgee* (a jeweled plume worn above the sirpesh). If you are sadly turbanless, and just have an ordinary hat, you can always attach a *cache-peigne*, a bow or ornament, which is usually worn at the back. You could also add a *bongrace*, 'a shade worn on the front of a bonnet or hat to protect the wearer's complexion from the sun.'

However, it's the men who really are spoiled for choice, at least in words *castorial* (related to hats). They can wear *jipijapas* (Panama hats), *lum-hats* (chimney-pot hats), *morions* (a kind of brimmed helmet resembling a hat, without a visor), a *copataine* or *copintank* (a high-crowned hat in the form of a sugar-loaf), a *nudger* (bowler hat), a *pakul* (a kind of flat round woolen hat traditionally worn in Afghanistan), a *balibuntal* (a hat made of very fine straw, as opposed to a *rusky*, a hat made of coarse straw), a *gibus* (an opera or crush hat), or even a *hattock* (a little hat).

If you happen to be an Italian sharpshooter, you could wear a *bersaglieri hat*, a hat with a dark plume of cock's feathers; if you are a policeman of a retro bent, you could wear a *sugarallie hat*, a tall cylindrical hat, formerly much worn by policemen. If you're neither sharpshooter nor policeman, but your work takes you to slightly less temperate climes, you could wear a *terai*, which the *OED* calls 'a wide-brimmed felt hat with double crown and special ventilation, worn in sub-tropical regions where the heat is not so intense as to necessitate the use of the sola topee or pith sun-helmet.' A *toering*, 'a wide-brimmed cone-shaped straw hat, formerly worn by Cape Malays,' might be useful if you go anywhere hotter.

If your pocketbook is a bit skint, you could always go for a *moloker*, a renovated silk hat, or a *muller*, a tall hat cut down into the low-crowned muller style. There's always the *demicastor*, too, made of inferior beaver, or of a mixture of beaver and other fur—perhaps you could leave the beaver out of it entirely and try a *mouldwarp hat*, made of moleskin.

If you are of an antiquarian bent, you could try a *kausia*, a felt hat worn by the ancient Macedonians, or the *petasus*, worn for traveling in ancient Greece (that's the hat Hermes is usually pictured wearing).

If you kelp a person, you move your hat to him, and if that hat is *chalked*, you are allowed to ride the railways for free, although you should keep your head (not to mention that hat) about you.

hatikvah [huh-**teek**-vah] the Israeli national anthem. It means 'the hope' in Hebrew.

haucepy [**hoh**-suh-pee] a kind of trap for wild animals, especially wolves. From a French word meaning 'to lift up the foot.'

hautain [haw-**tane**] an obsolete adjective meaning 'proud, arrogant,' or (of the voice) 'raised, loud.' From an Old French word meaning 'high.'

hebetude [**heb**-uh-t(y)ood] a literary word meaning 'dullness or lethargy.' It comes from a Latin adjective meaning 'blunt.'

heinsby [**haynz**-bee] an obsolete word defined in the *OED* as 'a mean wretch.' Possibly related to the verb *hain*, 'to keep from spending or consuming.'

heisenbug [**hye**-zuhn-bug] an error in a computer program that disappears or behaves differently when you attempt to fix or isolate it. Computing jargon, this word comes from Werner Heisenberg's Uncertainty Principle in quantum physics, the principle that the momentum and position of a particle cannot both be known precisely at the same time—the attempt to determine one makes it impossible to know the other.

hemianopsia [he-mee-uhn-**ahp**-see-uh] half-blindness, or loss of perception of one-half of the field of vision. Only used in the specialist sense to date, but crying out for a figurative use: "Whenever his parents fight his *hemianopsia* kicks in, and he's only able to see his father's side of the argument."

heptamerous [hep-**tam**-er-us] an adjective meaning 'having seven parts or members.'

herisson [**herr**-i-suhn] a structure like a wooden horse covered with spikes or points, used as a military punishment. The person being punished was made to ride it. It comes from a Latin word meaning 'hedgehog.'

heterarchy [**het**-er-ahr-kee] government by strangers or foreigners. Literally, 'rule of an alien,' which leaves itself open to so *many* jokes that I can't pick just one.

heterography [het-uh-**rah**-gruh-fee] an obsolete and rare word meaning 'incorrect spelling.' Also, *inorthography*. How much better to say, "I'm an *inorthographist*" than to admit you can't spell worth a damn?

hibernacle [**hye**-ber-nack-kle] a winter retreat, or the winter home of a hibernating animal. From a Latin word meaning 'wintry.' "I have a little *hibernacle* in Florida" is a lovely sentence from October through April.

hiccius doccius [**hick**-shee-us **dock**-shee-us] a word like 'abracadabra' or 'presto,' used by jugglers when performing tricks. By extension, a word for a juggler or someone who cuts corners. This may be a corruption of the Latin phrase *hicce est doctus* 'this is the learned man,' or perhaps just a nonsense phrase that sounds like Latin.

hierodule [**hye**-er-uh-d(y)ool] a slave who lives in a temple and is dedicated to the service of a god. *Heiro-* is a Greek root meaning 'holy' and shows up in a great many words, such as *hieromonarch*, 'a monk who is also a priest,' *hieromnemon*, 'a sacred recorder,' *hierography*, 'the description of religions,' and *hierophobia*, 'fear of sacred things.'

hippotomist [hi-**pah**-tuh-mist] an accomplished horse-dissector. *Hippo*- is the Greek root meaning 'horse,' and -tomy is a Greek root meaning 'cut.'

histrion [**his**-tree-un] an insulting term for an actor. An 1862 citation from the *OED* reads "It was found necessary to expel the *histrions*."

hodmandod [**hahd**-muhn-dahd] any strange person, a scarecrow. This word has the equally wonderful variants *hodmadod, hodmedod, hodman Hob*, and *hodmandon*.

hoddypeak [**hah**-dee-peek] an obsolete word meaning 'a fool or blockhead.'

hodograph [**hah**-doh-graff] a machine for registering the paces of a horse (to better tell one from another). From Greek words meaning 'way' and 'writing.'

hofles [**hofe**-liss] an obsolete word meaning 'excessive, unreasonable.' From an Old Norse word meaning 'immoderate.'

hoghenhine [**hoh**-guhn-hine] a member of one's family. It comes from *oen hine*, Middle English for 'own hind,' and was chiefly used in legal contexts. *Hind* is an old word for 'servant.'

hogo [**hoh**-goh] a stink. This comes from an anglicized spelling of the French haut *goût*, meaning 'high savor or flavor.'

holagogue [**hah**-luh-gog] a medicine that is supposed to get rid of all 'morbid humours.' (A lovely name for an antidepressant, if Big Pharma is listening.)

honeyfuggle [**huh**-nee-fuh-guhl]   to swindle, cheat. This word is American slang and apparently from *honey* plus *fugle*, meaning 'to cheat, trick.'

hongi [**hahng**-ee]   a traditional Maori greeting or salutation made by pressing or touching noses.

hookum-snivey [**hook**-um-**sniv**-ee]   any fakery or deceit. Also, any contraption used for unlocking a door from the outside (other than a key, of course).

houghmagandy [hahk-muh-**gan**-dee]   sexual intercourse with a person one is not married to. A rare word, it is found mainly in Scottish writing of the eighteenth and early nineteenth centuries, though it also appears in Vladimir Nabokov's *Pale Fire* (1962): "She would have preferred him to have gone through a bit of wholesome *houghmagandy* with the wench."

huderon [**hyoo**-der-un]   an obsolete adjective meaning 'lazy.' The singsongy citation from 1721 reads "a morning-sleep is worth a foldful of sheep to a huderon duderon Daw.' A *daw* is a sluggard; *duderon* is undefined and probably just reduplicative, as in *higgledy-piggledy*.

iatraliptic [eye-**at**-ruh-**lip**-tick] a doctor who cures diseases with lotions or creams. As an adjective, it means 'of or about the curing of diseases with lotions or creams.'

icasm [eye-**kazm**] a figurative expression. From a Greek word meaning 'to make like.'

ichneutic [ick-**n(y)oo**-tick] an adjective meaning 'relating to trackers or tracking.'

ichnography [ick-**nog**-ruh-fee] a floor-plan for a building. From Greek words meaning 'track' and 'writing.'

ichnomancy [ick-**noh**-mun-see] the science of making deductions about people and animals by examining their footsteps. The *OED* citation from 1855 seems to imply that you may find out "figure, peculiarities, occupations, &c, of men or beasts" by this method. From Greek words meaning 'track' and 'divination.'

ichoglan [**itch**-o-glan] a page waiting in the palace of the Sultan. From Turkish words that mean 'interior' and 'young man.' In this definition, 'waiting' obviously means 'serving,' but it's so much more poetic to understand it as 'to stay in expectation of.' What is he waiting *for*? Alas, the Sultan has fled, and we will never know.

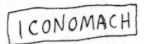

ichthyarchy [**ik**-thee-ar-kee] the domain of the fishes, the fish-world. A nonce-word used in 1853, but lovely in its ornate simplicity.

ichthyoallyeinotoxism [ick-thee-oh-al-ee-**ayn**-oh-**toks**-izm] a kind of food poisoning, which causes vivid and terrifying hallucinations in people who eat fish that have themselves eaten certain algae containing indoles, chemicals similar to LSD.

iconomicar [eye-kuh-**nah**-mi-ker] a writer about agriculture. A synonym (surprising that we need one) for *geoponic*.

iconomach [eye-**kah**-nuh-mak] a rare word meaning 'one who is hostile to images.'

icterical [ick-**terr**-i-kle] an adjective meaning 'tinged with yellow.' *Luteolous* is another adjective meaning 'yellowish.' *Flavescate* is a rare, obsolete adjective that means 'to make yellow.'

ideokinetic [eye-dee-oh-ki-**net**-ik] a kind of apraxia in which the sufferer still has the physical ability to perform an action or movement and understands a request to perform it, but is unable to do so when asked. This might be a good technical name for the common phenomenom of being able to perform astounding physical or mental feats, but not if anyone is watching.

idioticon [id-ee-**oh**-ti-kun] a dictionary of words used in one region only.

idolothyous [eye-duh-**lah**-thee-us] an adjective meaning 'sacrificed to an idol.' The noun is *idolothyte*, and the word *idolothytic* means 'characterized by the eating of meat sacrificed to idols.' Waste not, want not.

ignavy [ig-**nay**-vee] sluggish or slothful. From Latin meaning 'not busy.'

igarape [i-gah-rah-**pay**] in South America, a stream wide enough for a canoe.

ignicolist [ig-**nik**-uh-list] a fire-worshipper. *Ignivomous* is another uncommon word with the *igni*- 'fire' root; it means 'vomiting fire.' Perhaps a happy occasion if one worships fire, but otherwise not. *Ignivomous*, unsurprisingly, is mostly used literally about volcanoes and figuratively about foul-mouthed people.

ignify [**ig**-nee-fy] a rare word meaning 'to set on fire, to make burn.' The *OED* entry for this word contains this marvelous theory, in a quotation from 1659: "Falling-Stars . . . may be made either by pieces broken off from the true Stars . . . or from a company of ignifying Atoms, meeting and joining together to effect it."

ignimbrite [ig-**nihm**-brite] rock made from a *nuée adente*, the glowing cloud of ash, gas, and lava fragments ejected from a volcano. Ignimbrite is from Latin words meaning 'fire' and 'stormcloud': *nuée adente* is French for 'burning cloud.'

ignoscency [ig-**noh**-sun-see] a rare and obsolete word meaning 'forgiveness.' From a Latin word meaning 'to take no notice of.'

ignotism [**ig**-nuh-tiz-um] an obsolete word meaning 'a mistake due to ignorance.'

igry [**ig**-ree] painfully embarrassed by someone else's poor behavior. It can also be used to describe someone else's poor behavior. This word was invented by John Chaneski, Peter Gordon, Kevin West, and Francis Heaney, in part because they were annoyed by the *-gry* puzzle. The *-gry* puzzle ("Apart from *angry* and *hungry*, what other common English word ends in *-gry*?") is a broken puzzle—until *igry*, there was not another common word in English that ended in *-gry*. (And I suppose *igry* is not actually common yet.) The original puzzle was most likely something like "Think of words ending in *-gry*. *Angry* and *hungry* are two of them. What is the third word in the English language? You use it every day, and if you were listening carefully, I've just told you what it is." That puzzle is trying to get you to say *language* (i.e., the third word in the phrase "the English language") but someone broke it, and the broken version has been circulating on the Internet ever since. The Igry Men, avid puzzlers, decided to invent a new *-gry* word, so that when they were asked about the broken puzzle, they could say "Oh, it's *igry*, I thought everyone knew that word!" Perhaps someday everyone will.

ikbal [**ik**-bal] a member of the harem of an Ottoman sultan, especially a favorite of the Sultan.

illatration [il-uh-**tray**-shuhn] an act of barking at someone or something. This word is used figuratively but would be useful to make distinctions between dogs barking just to bark, and dogs barking at a particular thing or person (e.g., a car, a burglar, a mail carrier).

illecebrous [ill-**less**-uh-brus] an obsolete word meaning 'attractive, alluring.' From a Latin word meaning 'to entice.'

illeism [**il**-ee-iz-um] excessive reference to oneself in the third person; especially excessive use of the pronoun *he*.

illywhacker [**il**-ee-(h)wack-ur] an informal Australian word meaning 'a small-time confidence trickster.' It can be traced back to the 1940s, but its origin is unknown.

ilspile [**ill**-spill] a hedgehog. There are a surprising number of names for the hedgehog: *cirogrille* (actually a hyrax, but understood by medieval writers to be a hedgehog), *echinus* (Latin for hedgehog, but used as an English word by some early writers), *furze-pig, herisson, hotchi witchu* (the Romany name for the hedgehog), *hurcheon, irchepil, irspile, il* (or *ile*), *irchon* (or *irchin*), *tiggy*, and *urchin*.

imberb [im-**burb**] a rare adjective meaning 'beardless.' *Imberbic* is another form. It comes from *im-* plus the Latin *barba*, 'beard.'

imborsation [im-bor-**say**-shuhn] an Italian method of electing magistrates in which the names of the candidates are put in a bag and the winners are drawn out. The lone citation from the *OED* has eight hundred names being put in the purse but no mention of the number of magistrate-winners.

imbost [im-**boast**] the foam in 'foaming at the mouth.' The *OED* has it as 'foam from the mouth of a beast.' As a verb, it means to harass someone or something until they foam at the mouth, or to drive someone to madness.

imbriferous [im-**brif**-er-us] bringing rain; rainy. From a Latin word meaning 'a shower.'

immensikoff [i-**men**-si-kawf] a slang term for a heavy overcoat trimmed with fur, supposedly from "The Shoreditch Toff," a popular song from about 1868, in which there are the lines "I fancy I'm a toff, From top to toe I really think I looks—*Immensikoff*." (A *toff* is a stylish man.) The singer of the song, Arthur Lloyd, wore such an overcoat.

immerd [im-**murd**] a rare word meaning 'to cover something in dung or ordure.' From a Latin word meaning 'dung.'

immram [**im**-ram] a kind of Irish sea story in which the hero, along with a few boon companions, wanders from island to island having wonderful adventures. The best known recount the adventures of St. Brendan, who is also occasionally credited with having discovered America in his last voyage.

impaludism [im-**pal**-yoo-diz-um] a diseased state, including enlargement of the spleen and frequent fevers, found in marsh-dwellers. This is probably what we now call malaria (which comes from Italian 'bad air'). This word comes from the Latin for 'marsh.'

imparidigitate [im-parr-i-**didj**-i-tate] having an odd number of digits (toes or fingers) on each limb. The specific word for having an odd number of toes is *perissodactyl*. *Imparidigitate* comes from Latin for 'unequal' plus 'digit,' *perissodactyl* comes from the Greek for 'uneven' plus 'digit.'

impeticos [im-**pet**-i-kahs] a word written as dialogue to make a character seem foolish. From Shakespeare, *Twelfth Night* II. iii. 27, said by Feste. Apparently it is a form of *impocket*, 'put in one's pocket' and was perhaps intended to suggest *petticoat*.

> *Sir Andrew:* I sent thee sixe pence for thy leman, hadst it?
> *Feste:* I did impeticos thy gratillity.

impignorate [im-**pig**-nuh-rate] to pawn or mortgage something. This comes from a Latin word meaning 'to pledge.' To *repignorate* is to redeem a pledge.

impigrous [im-**pig**-grus] an obsolete and rare adjective meaning 'quick, diligent.' *Impigrity* is the noun; both come from *im-* and the Latin word *piger*, 'sluggish.'

impluvious [im-**ploo**-vee-us] a rare adjective meaning 'wet with rain.'

inaniloquent [in-an-**nill**-uh-kwunt] an obsolete and rare adjective meaning "full of idle talk, foolishly babbling." From Latin words meaning 'inane,' and 'to speak.' Other forms include *inaniloquous, inaniloquence,* and *inaniloquation.*

incompt [in-**kahmpt**] an obsolete adjective meaning 'messy, inelegant.' From a Latin word meaning 'unadorned, rough.'

incontunded [in-kun-**tun**-did] an obsolete adjective meaning 'not bruised or pounded.' One would hope this would be an adjective applicable to all people, everywhere, all the time. It seems to be used mostly about spices and fruit.

indagatrix [in-duh-**gay**-triks] an obsolete and rare word meaning 'a female searcher or investigator.' It is the feminine of the Latin word *indagator*, meaning 'a tracer, an investigator.'

infelicific [in-fee-luh-**sif**-ik] an adjective meaning 'making unhappy.' This is mostly used in the discussion of ethics, with citations like "The breach of any moral rule is pro tanto *infelicific* from its injurious effects on moral habits generally."

inficete [in-fuh-**seet**] a rare adjective meaning 'unfacetious, not witty.' One of the citations from the *OED*, from Thomas Love Peacock's novel of *Crotchet Castle* (1831), is this lovely exchange:

> *Mr. E.:* Sir, you are very facetious at my expense.
> *Dr. F.:* Sir, you have been very unfacetious, very inficete at mine.

influous [**in**-floo-us] an obsolete and rare adjective meaning 'shedding astral influence.' In other words, what you do when your horoscope for the day is bad and you resolve to take no notice of it.

infrendiate [in-**fren**-dee-ate] to gnash the teeth. It almost makes you *infrendiate* just to say it.

infucate [**in**-fyoo-kate] to use makeup. Earlier definitions were 'to paint the face, to color the face artificially.' The word sounds as impious and obscene as the practice was thought to be! The noun is even worse: *infucation*.

inhebetate [in-**heb**-i-tate] to make something dull or blunt. Everyone knows a person who can *inhebetate* the most exciting story. Unfortunately.

inhume [in-**hyoom**] a poetic verb meaning 'to bury someone or something.' The word for the reverse process, *exhume*, is rather more familiar in current English: both come from a Latin word for 'ground.'

inunct [in-**ungkt**] a very rare word meaning 'to apply ointment to someone or something.'

iotacist [eye-**oh**-tuh-sist] someone who makes excessive use of the letter *i*. Originally meaning the changing of the pronunciation of other Greek vowels to be more like the pronunciation of the vowel *iota*, this word could have a new use as a way to refer to someone boastful and self-centered.

isangelous [eye-**san**-djuh-lus] an obsolete and rare adjective meaning 'equal to the angels.' The citation from the *OED* is "Let us look back upon ourselves, who we expect shall one day be made *isangelous*, equal to the angels."

isocephaly [eye-soh-**sef**-uh-lee] the principle observed in some ancient Greek reliefs, especially in friezes, of representing the heads of all the figures at nearly the same level. (This is often now done in movies or at press conferences to give the illusion of all the participants being the same height.)

isocracy [eye-**sah**-kruh-see] a system of government in which all the people possess equal political power. The citation in the *OED* from 1652 shows that we have always been cynical about the practicality of this idea: "It remaineth doubtfull, whether people who live together, may lawfully retain an *Isocracie* among them." An *isocrat* is an advocate of *isocracy*; to *isocratize* is to practice *isocracy*. The equality of people before the law, or the equality of political rights among the citizens of a state, is *isonomy*.

INTRIGUING AND INCREDIBLE -IST WORDS

The handy suffix *-ist* has found its way onto many a weird and wonderful word. Of course, if you are an *acosmist*, you deny the existence of the universe, which also lets out any belief in the suffix *-ist*.

If you're an *adiabolist*, you don't believe in the existence of a devil, although it's possible to at the same time be a *diablerist*, someone who paints or draws pictures in which devils appear. A *demonurgist* is someone who practices magic with the help of demons (it's much easier, I guess, with a few extra hands to hold things, and to fill out the chanting). An *energumenist* is one possessed by a demon, or someone who is a fanatical enthusiast for something.

A *battologist* has nothing to do with bats, in the ordinary way of things—instead he or she needlessly repeats the same thing, needlessly, needlessly. *Biloquists* can speak in two different voices (if they are also *gastriloquists*, one of those voices will seem to come from their bellies). A *heterophemist* is someone who says something other than what he or she meant to say. (I hope never to meet a heterophemic biloquistical gastriloquist.) A *neoterist* is someone who favors new words and expressions. A *phlyarologist* is someone who 'talks nonsense'. A *querulist* is someone who complains (*a lot* is implied).

We would all like to feel that we are *antisocordists*, opponents of sloth or stupidity, although it's more likely that we are *inadvertists*, people who 'habitually fail to take notice,' or are consistently oblivious. A *crinanthropist* is someone who 'judges mankind' (and most likely finds it wanting). A *malist* is someone who believes that this world, though not the worst possible world, is still pretty bad. A *psychrolutist* is someone who recommends cold baths, and a *carcerist* is someone who advocates prisons, although it's likely there's a lot of overlap between those two groups.

A *cereologist* is someone who investigates crop circles (at significant risk of alien abduction). A *fumifugist* is someone who drives away smoke (or, perhaps, someone who drives away smokers). A *heartist* is a fencer who can pierce the heart (with an actual sword, not with words or melting glances). A *bouquinist* is a dealer in secondhand books of little value. A *pyrgologist* is someone who is an expert in the history and structure of towers. A *tziganologist* studies Hungarian gypsies.

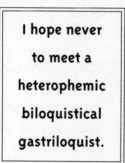

I hope never to meet a heterophemic biloquistical gastriloquist.

An *Exarchist* is someone who supports the Exarch of Bulgaria against the Patriarch of Constantinople, come what may. An *elaterist* is someone who explains certain phenomena as being due to the elasticity of the air. (Good enough for me.) A *gymnobiblist* is someone who believes that the unannotated text of the Bible is enough of a guide to religious truth for even the least-educated person. A *juredivinist* is a believer in the divine right of kings. A *chorizontist* is someone who believes (most likely with fanatical enthusiasm) that the *Iliad* and the *Odyssey* were the fruits of different authors, and thus is more than likely someone you do not want to be seated next to at dinner.

A *nuxodeltiologist* is someone who collects postcards that show nighttime scenes. An *exonumist* is someone who collects things that look like coins, but aren't. I haven't found a word for someone who collects -*ist* words; coinages gratefully accepted care of the publisher.

iteroparous [it-er-**rah**-per-us] an adjective used to describe organisms that have multiple sets of offspring, or that give birth more than once during the organism's life cycle. An organism that reproduces only once during its life is *semelparous,* a plant that fruits only once and dies is *monocarpic.* The *iter-* here is the same *iter-* as in *iteration; semel-* comes from a Latin word meaning 'once.'

ithand [**eye**-thund] an obsolete Scottish word meaning 'diligent, busy,' or 'uninterrupted.' Which makes this word its own antonym, because busy people are constantly interrupted, usually by someone who stands in the doorway saying "I know you're busy, but . . . ."

ithyphallic [ith-ee-**fal**-ik] an adjective meaning 'indecent, obscene,' from association with its other meaning, 'having an erect phallus.' It comes from the practice of carrying a phallus (a model, one hopes) in procession at festivals of Bacchus. The *ithy-* part comes from a Greek word meaning 'straight.' The implication that curved phalli were also used is not borne out by the etymological record, as there is no word in the *OED* meaning 'curved phallus.'

J

jackeen [jak-**een**] an Anglo-Irish word used to describe someone evidently worthless, but who nevertheless feels he is very important.

jactance [**jack**-tunce] a rare word meaning 'boasting.'

jaculiferous [jack-yuh-**lif**-er-us] an adjective meaning 'having prickles.' Could certainly be used to replace the overworn "He's got a chip on his shoulder the size of Texas!"

jannock [**jan**-uk] a dialect adjective meaning 'fair, genuine.' It's one of those words used frequently in the negative, as in "that's not *jannock!*" Also used as an adverb: "Act *jannock*, or else I'll turn this car around, I swear!"

jargogle [**jar**-goh-gle] an obsolete verb meaning 'to confuse, to mix up.' The probable adjective, *jargogled*, sounds almost onomatopoeic.

jau dewin [**jaw** duh-**win**] a term of reproach, of obscure origin, from the late 1300s. No matter what the origin, we can always use another term of reproach.

javanais [zhah-vah-**nay**] a French slang, like pig Latin, in which *av* or *va* is introduced after each syllable or word.

jectigation [jeck-ti-**gay**-shun] a wagging or trembling movement. From a Latin word meaning 'to throw.'

jentation [jen-**tay**-shun] a rare and obsolete word meaning 'breakfast.' Also, *jenticulation*. *Jenticulate* is the verb, meaning 'to breakfast.'

jettatura [jet-uh-**toor**-uh] the evil eye, bad luck. From an Italian word meaning 'person who brings bad luck.' A citation in the *OED* from the *Glasgow Herald* of 1921 says, "This simple remedy is much in use throughout Italy to-day as an antidote to the evil power of the *Jettatore*." Annoyingly, and dangerously, the remedy is not named.

jiffle [**jif**-uhl] to fidget or shuffle. This is just one of several words that can mean 'fidget' and end in -*le*, including *figgle*, *fissle*, *nestle*, *sessle*, *tiddle*, and *trifle*.

jirble [**jur**-ble] to spill liquid by unsteady movement of the container; to pour liquid from vessel to vessel. Of onomatopoeic origin.

jocoserious [joh-koh-**sear**-ee-us] half jocular, half serious; partly silly and partly somber; blending jokes and serious matters. The noun, used only once, is *jocoseriosity*.

joinpee [**join**-pee] an obsolete and rare adjective meaning 'with the feet joined or put close together.'

jollop [**joll**-up] to make a noise like a turkey. As a noun it means 'the cry of a turkey.' Unfortunately, it doesn't seem to have been used in any Thanksgiving poetry.

jollux [**joll**-uks] an obsolete slang term meaning 'a fat person.'

jumentous [joo-**men**-tuhs] a very rare adjective meaning 'resembling horse's urine.' In the nineteenth century, the Sydenham Society's Lexicon of Medicine and Allied Sciences defined this word as 'a term applied to urine which is high colored, strong smelling, and turbid, like that of the horse.' It comes from *jument*, an obsolete word that means 'a beast of burden.'

kaibun [**kye**-bun] a Japanese palindrome. Since Japanese is not an alphabetic language, the units being reversed are not letters but moras, and are usually phrases or sentences and not single words (although single-word *kaibun* are possible). A famous *kaibun* is "Na-ru-to wo to-ru-na" (Do not take my *naruto* [spiral-shaped fishcake]). Because Japanese is written vertically, *kaibun* are not the same "backwards and forwards" but the same when read from the top or the bottom.

kakistocracy [kack-i-**stah**-kruh-see] the government of a state by its worst citizens. The adjective is *kakistocratical*. A lovely piece of rhetoric is the 1876 citation in the *OED:*

> Is ours a government of the people, by the people, for the people, or a Kakistocracy rather, for the benefit of knaves at the cost of fools?

kalokagathia [kal-oh-kuh-**gath**-ee-uh] nobility and goodness of character. From Greek words meaning 'beautiful' and 'good,' describing the perfect character.

kamagraphy [kuh-**mag**-ruh-fee] the process of making copies of paintings, using a special press and treated canvas, which reproduces exactly the color and texture of the original brushstrokes. However, the citations seem to suggest that it destroys the original painting in the process, so it's not exactly what the counterfeiters and forgers of the world have been waiting for.

karmadharaya [kahr-muh-**dahr**-ee-uh] a compound word in which the first part of the word describes the second, such as *highway* (adjective + noun) or *steamboat* (attributive noun + noun). From *karma* plus a Sanskrit word meaning 'holding, bearing.'

karoshi [kuh-**roh**-shee] death caused by overwork or job-related exhaustion. A Japanese term, it came into general use in the late 1980s, although it is still used only in the context of workers in Japan. It derives from words meaning 'excess,' 'labor,' and 'death.'

katsuramono [kaht-soo-rah-**moh**-noh] one of the types of Japanese Noh drama, in which the chief character is female and the theme romantic. It is usually presented as the third play in a performance of Noh. A man who plays female roles in Kabuki drama is known as an *onnagata* or *oyama*.

katavothron [kat-uh-**vah**-thrun] a subterranean channel or deep chasm formed by running water. From Greek words meaning 'swallow' and 'hole.'

kathenotheism [kath-**en**-oh-thee-iz-um] a kind of polytheism where each god is single and supreme in turn. From a Greek word meaning 'one by one' and -*theism.*

kebbie [**keb**-ee] a staff with a hooked head, like a shepherd's crook.

kench [kentch] an obsolete and rare word meaning 'to laugh loudly.'

kenodoxy [**kee**-nuh-dock-see] an obsolete and rare word meaning 'the love or study of boasting or vainglory.'

kenspeckle [**ken**-spek-uhl] a Scottish word meaning 'conspicuous, easily recognizable.' The origin is not precisely known, but it may be related to a Swedish word meaning 'quick at recognizing people or things.'

kishen [**kish**-un] a measure used on the Isle of Man, containing eight quarts. In the *OED*, the measured commodities are oats and potatoes; ale and coal also comes in *kishens*. A *kishen* of potatoes, it is said, should weigh twenty-one pounds, a *kishen* of coal slightly more.

kleptolagnia [klep-to-**lag**-nee-uh] the desire to reach sexual gratification through theft. From Greek words meaning 'thief' and 'lust.'

knabble [**nab**-ul] an obsolete word meaning 'to bite or nibble.' A Google check of this word turns it up on a list that calls itself "The finest and longest collection of hamster names in the WWW!", which seems appropriate.

knackatory [**nack**-uh-tor-ee] an obsolete and rare word meaning 'a place to buy knick-knacks.' (It sounds more like a place of punishment for those who bestow too many knick-knacks upon others. "That's the third vase this year! Off to the *knackatory* with you!")

knaifatic [nay-uh-**fat**-ick] an adjective meaning 'knavish' or 'low-born.' In the *OED* it is labeled as obsolete, Scottish, and a nonce-word, which is surprising as you would think that the opportunities to call someone *knaifatic* would be plentiful in sixteenth-century Scotland.

knilb [nilb] opening your eyes and then closing them again quickly. A knilb is the opposite of a blink, and is *blink* spelled backwards.

kinnikinnick [ki-ni-ki-**nik**] a substance consisting of dried sumac leaves and willow or dogwood bark, smoked by North American Indians as a tobacco substitute or mixed together with tobacco. The word comes from Unami, an extinct Algonquian language, in which its meaning was 'mixture.'

korrigan [**kor**-ee-gun] in Breton folklore, a fairy or witch who steals children.

krobylos [**kra**-by-lahs] in Greek art, a knot or bun of hair on the top of the head.

kurdaitcha [kuh-**dye**-chuh] an Australian word for a malignant supernatural being, taken from the word for the shoes worn to ward off such a creature. The shoes were made of the feathers of an emu stuck together with human blood.

kye [kie] a miserly sailor. Of unknown origin, but possibly related to a dialect word, *kyish*, meaning 'dirty.'

kyriolexy [**kye**-ree-oh-leck-see] the use of literal expressions. From Greek words meaning 'proper' and 'speaking.'

lacustrine [luh-**kus**-trin] an adjective meaning 'associated with lakes.' Taken from the Latin word for lake, it is used chiefly in technical contexts, as in *lacustrine sediments* or *lacustrine fish*.

laetificant [lit-**tiff**-i-kunt] a rare adjective meaning 'antidepressant, cheering.' Usually used about medicine.

lambdacism [**lam**-duh-siz-um] too frequent use of the letter *l* in speaking or writing. Also, pronouncing the letter *r* as the letter *l* (also called *lallation*).

langsuir [**lang**-soo-er] a female vampire that preys on newborn children. The langsuir (a Malayan monster) wears a green robe, has long black hair that covers the hole on the back of her neck (through which she sucks the blood of children), emits a whinnying cry, and can take the shape of an owl. All in all, a terrifying creature. Another Malay vampire is the *penanggalan*, which also preys on newborns but has the form of a human head with a stomach sac attached.

leathwake [**leeth**-wake] an obsolete word meaning 'having flexible joints, lithe.' From Old English words meaning 'limb' and 'soft.'

leggiadrous [ledj-ee-**add**-rus] an obsolete and rare adjective meaning 'graceful, elegant.' From an Italian word meaning 'sprightly.'

leguleian [leg-yoo-**lee**-an] an adjective meaning 'pertaining petty or unimportant questions of law.' As a noun it means 'a pettifogging lawyer.'

lerky [**ler**-kee] a children's game in which all the players but one hide and a tin can is placed in a ring. The players then try to kick the can out of the ring without being seen.

lethiferous [li-**thif**-er-us] causing death, deadly. From Latin words meaning 'death' and 'bring.'

libant [**lye**-bant] an adjective meaning 'tasting, lightly touching.' This word is related to *libation*; they both come from a Latin word meaning 'to taste.'

limbeck [**lim**-beck] to wear yourself out in the effort to have a new idea. This word ultimately comes from an Arabic word meaning 'a still,' the analogy being that you distill ideas with your brain.

limerence [**lim**-er-uhns] the initial exhilarating rush of falling in love; the state of being in love. This word was coined by Dorothy Tennov in a 1979 book titled *Love and Limerence*. Psychologists have found that this state lasts for an average of three years.

limicolous [li-**mi**-kuh-luhs] living in mud. Usually applied to birds or worms, this word comes from Latin words meaning 'mud' and 'to inhabit.' A related adjective is *limicoline*. Something that lives in the open part of a freshwater lake or pond, not near the muddy edges or bottom, is *limnetic*, from a Greek word meaning 'living in marshes.'

limitanean [lim-i-**tay**-nee-un] an adjective meaning 'on the border.' A term from Roman antiquity, it usually refers to soldiers stationed on the border. Another similar word is *limitrophe*, an adjective meaning 'on the frontier.'

linguipotence [ling-**gwip**-uh-tunce] mastery of languages or the tongue. A nonce word used once by Samuel Taylor Coleridge: "The New Testament contains not the least proof of the *linguipotence* of the Apostles, but the clearest proof of the contrary."

lipothymia [li-puh-**thy**-mee-uh] fainting or swooning. One of the citations in the *OED* reads "Others are freed from *lypothymias* by being pinched, or having cold water thrown in their faces."

liripoop [**li**-ri-poop] the tail of a graduate's hood (an archaic feature of academic dress). The *liripoop* (etymology unknown) hung down the back when the hood was off, and it was wrapped like a bandage around the head when the hood was on. Like most academic dress, the *liripoop* is both intimidating to others and uncomfortable for the wearer.

logion [**log**-ee-on] a traditional saying or proverb of a sage. Chiefly used with reference to the sayings of Jesus contained in the collections supposed to have been among the sources of the Gospels, or to sayings attributed to Jesus but not recorded in the Gospels. From a Greek word meaning 'oracle.'

logodaedaly [lah-guh-**dee**-duh-lee] ingenious or cunning use of words. *Logo-* comes from a Greek root meaning 'word,' and *-daedaly* is related to *Daedalus*, the name of the designer of the Labyrinth for the Minotaur of Crete. His name has come to mean 'ingenious, skillful.' Another rare *logo-* word is the nonce-word *logopandocie*, which is the 'readiness to admit words of all kinds' and describes the English language (and most lexicographers).

logomachy [luh-**gah**-muh-kee] fighting about words, a fight about words. From Greek words meaning 'word' and 'fighting.' This kind of fight is always all heat and no light.

lolling-lobby [**lohl**-ing-**lob**-ee] an obsolete and derisory term for a monk. Perhaps not so many people have occasion to abuse monks today as in the past, so that the word has fallen into disrepair. The word is perhaps from *loll-in-lobby*, but that form has not been found.

longicorn [**lahn**-ji-korn] a kind of beetle with very long antennae. The word comes from Latin words meaning 'long' and 'horn,' and it is a good example of a word with a perfectly serviceable etymology that still sounds made-up.

longinquity [lahn-**jing**-kwi-tee] a rare word meaning 'long distance, remoteness.' From a Latin word meaning 'long, distant.'

loon-slatt [**loon**-slat] an obsolete slang name for an old Scottish coin worth thirteen pence halfpenny, the proverbial amount of the hangman's fee.

LEARNED AND
LAUDABLE -LOGIES

The suffix -*logy*, from a Greek word meaning 'discourse, speak,' has been applied to form the names of all manner of sciences, both practical and absurd.

There's *balneology*, the medical study of bathing, and *escapology*, the study of the methods and technique of escaping. *Garbology*, the study of garbage as a social science, is probably more than tangentially related to *loimology*, the study of pestilential diseases. Someone who studies giants is interested in *gigantology*; and the study of mummies is *momiology*. The study of giant mummies, if there is such a thing, could be *gigantomomiology*. *Ptochology* is the study of unemployment and poverty (unfortunately a very rich field) and *squalorology* is the study of squalor. Once you're done with squalor (although a fascinating subject) you could move on to *acology*, the study of the methods of curing disease. Or to *anatripsology*, the study of the uses of friction. Or further still to *barology*, the study of weight, or *cyesiology*, the study of pregnancy, or *emmenology*, the study of menstruation. The study of hypnotism is *neurypnology*. The study of the sense of smell is *osphresiology*.

The study of the history of existing animals is *cainozoology*, as opposed to the investigation of the history of extinct animals, which is *paleozoology*. The study of imaginary animals would be, possibly, *phantastizoology*, but that word itself is imaginary. The study of fossil footprints is *ichnology*. The study of apparently useless rudimentary organs of plants and animals is *dysteleology*.

Of course, you could just throw in the towel on all the other *-logies* and devote yourself solely to *agnoiology,* the investigation into the character and conditions of ignorance. Or you could study *oudenology,* the science of things having no real existence (from a Greek root meaning 'nothing' and *-ology*). It might just be your lot to dabble in *deontology,* the science of duty and moral obligation, or *hamartiology,* the study of sin, or *ponerology,* the science of evil, or *heortology,* the study of the feasts of the Christian year. You could also engage in *naology,* the study of sacred buildings.

The study of slugs is *limacology.* (The *lima bean* is not related, being named for the capital of Peru.) The study of cooking is *magirology.* The study of entrails is *splanchnology,*

The study of giant mummies, if there is such a thing, could be *gigantomomiology.*

which sounds onomatopoeic but is not. The science of spirit-rapping (as in seances) is *typtology.* The science of joining (as in rivets, not in social clubs) is *zygology.*

There are many *-logies* that begin with *P.* The study of the origin of personal names is *patronomatology.* The science of counter-espionage is *phylactology.* The study of rivers is *potamology.* The scientific study of the face is *prosopology.* The study of the art of artillery is *pyroballogy.*

If none of these sciences interest you, you could begin your study of *pantology,* the systematic view of all branches of knowledge. Good luck!

loranthaceous [lor-un-**thay**-shus] a botanical adjective that means 'related to the mistletoe family.' This word fills a gap to describe kisses given (or received) in unusual circumstances, such as under the mistletoe.

lopeholt [**lope**-hohlt] an obsolete word meaning 'a refuge, a place of safety.' Possibly from Dutch words meaning 'run' and 'hollow.'

lordswike [**lord**-swick-uh] a person who deceives their lord, a traitor. From old English words meaning 'lord' and 'deceiver.'

loutrophoros [loo-troh-**for**-us] a tall vessel with two handles, used in ancient Greece to carry water to the nuptial bath. They were also put on the tombs of unmarried people. From Greek words meaning 'water for a bath' and 'carrying.'

lubitorium [loo-bi-**tor**-ee-uhm] a service station. This word apparently comes from *lubricate* plus the suffix *–torium* (as in *auditorium*).

lucifugous [loo-**sif**-yuh-gus] an adjective meaning 'shunning the light.' From Latin words meaning 'light' and 'to flee.' This was usually used as a near synonym for 'nocturnal' but seems much more poetic; instead of seeking the night, they are shunning the light. A similar adjective is *lucifugal*.

luculence [**loo**-kyoo-lunce] an obsolete and rare adjective meaning 'fineness, beauty,' or 'clearness, certainty.' From a Latin word meaning 'light.'

LORDSWIKE

ludibrious [loo-**dib**-ree-us] an obsolete adjective meaning 'likely to be the butt of a joke.' It can also mean 'scornful, scoffing.' It seems that one word covers all necessities: first you are made the object of mockery, and then you cover your hurt by scorning the mockers. From a Latin word meaning 'to play.'

LYSSOPHOBIA

luer [**loo**-er] a mechanical connection and seal used in medical machinery, especially IVs and other devices needing air- or watertight seals.

luscition [loo-**si**-shuhn] poor eyesight. This comes from a Latin word meaning 'one-eyed.'

lushburg [**lush**-berg] a counterfeit coin, made to look like an English silver penny, imported from Luxembourg during the reign of Edward III. *Lushberg* is an anglicization of *Luxembourg*.

lychnoscope [**lick**-nuh-scope] a name given to a small window, lower than the other windows, that is found in some old churches. Supposedly, the window was placed low so that the lepers outside could see the altar lights (lepers were obviously not allowed in the church itself). From Greek words meaning 'lamp' and 'look at.'

lycophosed [**lye**-kuh-fozed] an obsolete adjective meaning 'having keen sight.' From a Greek word meaning 'twilight,' from roots meaning 'wolf' and 'light,' which was misunderstood as 'having keen sight, like a wolf.'

lyssophobia [lis-o-**foh**-bee-uh] a fear of rabies so extreme that the sufferer actually manifests symptoms of the disease. This word comes from a Greek word meaning 'rabies' and the suffix *-phobia*.

macellarious [mass-uh-**lair**-ee-us] an obsolete adjective meaning 'like a butcher's' or 'like a slaughterhouse or shambles.' From a Latin word meaning 'meat market.' Perhaps the word could be renewed etymologically and be used to describe any place that exists only to encourage people to find romantic partners.

machicolation [muh-chick-uh-**lay**-shun] the opening in a wall through which fire, molten lead, stones, etc., are dropped on besiegers or attackers. Also used to mean the action of putting such things out of a machicolation.

macilent [**mas**-i-luhnt] an adjective meaning both 'thin' (as in weight) and 'lacking in substance' (as in worth), ideal for giving ambiguous compliments.

mackabroin [**mak**-uh-broin] an obsolete and rare word meaning 'an old hag.' It probably does not come from *macabre*, whose origin is obscure. The word did come from French, but whether the French word came from *Maccabeus* (as in Judas Maccabeus) or from another name is not known.

macushla [muh-**koosh**-luh] an affectionate form of address, used in Irish English. It comes from the Irish words *mo*, meaning 'my,' and *cuisle*, 'pulse'; a similar Irish word is *acushla*, from the phrase *a chuisle (moi chroi)*, 'O pulse (of my heart)!'

macroseism [**mack**-roh-sye-zum] a major earthquake, or any earth-quake that can be felt. Not in common use, because of the existence of the handy term 'earthquake.' *Seism* is another word that means 'earth-quake.' *Macroseismic* is an adjective used to describe those effects of an earthquake that can be detected without instruments (such as buildings collapsing, pictures falling off walls, etc.) From a Greek word meaning 'to shake.' Words not derived from Greek that mean 'earthquake' include *earth-din, earth-grine* or *earth-grith, earthquave,* and *terremote.*

macrosmatic [mack-rahz-**mat**-ik] an adjective meaning 'having well-developed olfactory organs.' Also used figuratively, as in this citation from the *OED* (where the subject is George Orwell): "[he is] a *macros-matic* writer tracking down the stench of hypocrisy or the gangrene of intellectual treachery." From *macro-* plus a Greek word meaning 'smell.'

magirology [madj-uh-**rah**-luh-djee] a rare word meaning 'the art or science of cooking.' A *magirist* (or *magirologist*) is an expert cook; something that is *magiristic* is related to cooking or cookery, and some-one that is *magirological* is skilled in cooking. From a Greek word meaning 'cook.'

magnolious [mag-**noh**-lee-us] a slang word meaning 'great, splendid, magnificent, large.'

magnoperate [mag-**nah**-puh-rate] to work on one's magnum opus. Used in a letter by Lord Byron: "That is right, keep to your magnum opus—*magnoperate* away."

maisterel [**mays**-ter-ell] a rare and obsolete term for an imp or famil-iar. Perhaps from Middle French *maistral,* meaning 'servant.'

majoun [muh-**joon**] an intoxicating Middle Eastern candy made of cannabis, ghee, honey, and spices.

malagrugrous [mal-uh-**groo**-grus] an obsolete humorous Scots word meaning 'dismal, doleful.' Likely from an old Irish word meaning 'wrinkle,' as in a furrowed brow. This word might have influenced the Scots word *malagruze*, which means 'to harm physically, to disorder.'

malandryn [mal-**an**-drin] a rare and obsolete word meaning 'robber, highwayman.' It's probably from a Latin word for a kind of rash that affects both horses and people, the idea being that disease and robbers are both nuisances.

mammothrept [**mam**-o-thrept] a spoiled child. This wonderful word comes from a Greek word meaning 'raised by one's grandmother.'

marcescible [mahr-**ses**-i-buhl] an adjective meaning 'tending or likely to wither or fade.' From a Latin word meaning 'to be faint.'

marrowsky [muh-**row**-skee] a kind of slang or error in speaking in which there is a transposition of the first letters, syllables, or parts of two words. Sadly, the notion that this word comes from the name of the Polish count Joseph Boruwlaski (1739–1837), who was a famous dwarf living in Britain, is called "unsupported" by the *OED*.

mascaron [**mas**-kuh-run] an image of a (usually grotesque) face, human or animal, used as an architectural ornament.

materteral [muh-**ter**-ter-uhl] an adjective meaning 'like an aunt.' Usually used humorously, it comes from a Latin word meaning 'maternal aunt.' (*Maternal* in the sense of being related through one's mother, not in the sense of 'motherly feeling,' although that is what is implied by the word *materteral.*)

matranee [muh-**trah**-nee] in India, a female servant who has to do all the nastiest work. One can hear thousands of Indian mothers saying to ungrateful offspring, "What do you think I am, your *matranee*?"

meacock [**mee**-kahk] a coward or effeminate person. The word is rarely found after the eighteenth century, although the *OED* does have one example of its use in 1921, from *Ulysses* by James Joyce. Its origin is unknown.

medkniche [**med**-nitch] a bundle of hay, usually measured as being as much as the hayward could lift with his middle finger as high as his knee. It was one of the perks of being the hayward, whose job was to keep the cows out of the common fields.

megacryometeor [meg-uh-kry-oh-**mee**-tee-ur] a large chunk of ice that falls from the sky, often without a clear cause or origin.

meliturgy [**mel**-i-ter-jee] honey-making or bee-keeping. From a Greek word meaning 'bee-keeping.'

mesonoxian [mezz-uh-**nock**-see-un] of or related to midnight. "What are your *mesonoxian* plans?" sounds so much better on December 31 than "Hey, whatcha doin' tonight?"

methysis [**meh**-thi-sis] an obsolete and rare word meaning 'addiction to drink' or 'habitual drunkenness.' From a Greek word meaning 'drunkenness.'

milce-witter [**mils**-wi-ter] an adjective meaning 'knowing mercy.' A similar adjective is *milce-hearted.*

milliad [**mil**-ee-ad] a thousand years. Formed (the *OED* used to say 'badly' but it no longer editorializes about this word) from *mille,* Latin for 'one thousand,' on the example of *myriad.*

mivvy [**miv**-ee] a derogatory word for a woman who runs a boarding-house. Another sense of *mivvy* is 'an expert.' You could be called a *mivvy mivvy,* if you were really good at running a boardinghouse.

moirologist [moy-**rah**-luh-jist] in Greece, a hired mourner. From Greek words meaning 'death' or 'fate' and 'speaker.' The moirologists may sing *myriologues,* extemporaneous funeral songs usually sung by women.

molendinarious [muh-len-duh-**nair**-ee-us] an obsolete adjective meaning 'of or pertaining to a mill.' *Molinology* is the study of mills and milling, which is of course done by *molinologists,* who pursue their *molinological* ends. *Molinary* means 'of or pertaining to the grinding of grain,' and someone who pays to have something ground at a mill is a *multurer.*

moliminous [moh-**lim**-uh-nus] an obsolete adjective meaning 'taking great effort, laborious.' Also, 'massive, momentous.' From a Latin word meaning 'effort.'

momurdotes [**moh**-mer-dotes] an obsolete word meaning 'the sulks.' The first part of this word may be imitative of mumbling or murmuring; the second part comes from *dote*, meaning 'to be silly, to act stupidly.'

monarsenous [mahn-**ahr**-suh-nuhs] this word does not mean, as one might think, 'having only one arse'; instead it means 'having only one male for several females.' Used mostly in zoological contexts, it seems apt for unbalanced dinner parties or junior-high dances. (In which case, perhaps the 'arse' interpretation could be revived, depending on the behavior of the male attendees.)

monkey's wedding [**mung**-keez-**wed**-ing] simultaneous rain and sunshine. This informal South African term probably comes from a Portuguese expression translated as 'vixen's wedding,' which has the same meaning, but there is also a possibility that it entered South African English from a Zulu phrase.

morate [**moh**-rate] an obsolete adjective meaning 'well mannered, moral, respectable.'

morfound [**mor**-fownd] (of horses and other animals) to be chilled, to be numb with cold. From French roots meaning 'mucus' and 'melt.'

morigerate [muh-**ridj**-er-it] a rare adjective meaning 'obedient.' The noun is *morigeration*, which had the extended meaning of 'obsequiousness.' The fine shading of how and when obedience becomes obsequiousness we leave to those experts in discerning it: teachers of adolescents.

MIGHTY AND
MARVELOUS MONEY

The love of money may be the root of all evil, but it's also the root of some very interesting weird and wonderful words. There are quite a few words for people who love money, especially those who lend it to others: *danists* and *fenerators* are usurers, *mahujuns*, *soucars*, *nummularians*, and *ockerers* are moneylenders, and *collybists* are both, and misers as well. A *wisseler* is a moneychanger, and *wissel* is change for an amount of money. Lending money at usury is *gombeenism*.

Lending at interest (or *fenory*) is not the only way to make money with money. You can also literally *make* money by indulging in *fausonry* (forgery). *Shoful* is counterfeit money. To *shroff* is to separate genuine coins from counterfeit, and *shroffage* is the commission charged for doing so. If you have some good coins lying around you can shave off a bit of the valuable metal here and there, resulting in *abatude*, clipped money. It's probably easier to shave off some of the *adminicles*, the decorations that surround the main figure on a coin. If you just want to melt the whole batch down and separate the silver from the alloy, you can practice *dealbation*.

Stealing money also has a wide vocabulary. A *defalcation* is an amount of money misappropriated by someone who is in charge of it, maybe by using the *salami technique*, in which small amounts of money are transferred from many customer accounts into another account held under a false name. And there's always *chevisance*, raising money by pawning something (also, any [bad] method of raising money), or *chantage*, blackmail. A sophisticated kind of blackmail is that of the Japanese *sokaiya*, who holds a small number of shares of stock in a number of companies and attempts to extort money from them by threatening to cause trouble at the general meeting of the stockholders. Perhaps the truly desperate can go on the *kinchin-lay*, and take money from children sent on errands.

Earning money by the sweat of your brow, while not an appealing option to everyone, has its proponents. Earning by the sweat of other people's brows has many more. If you're a bishop, you can sit back and receive your *senage*, or tribute, at Easter. Technically, this doesn't make the bishop a *gyesite*, some-

> **Perhaps the truly desperate can go on the *kinchin-lay*, and take money from children sent on errands.**

one who accepts money in return for spiritual things (considered as a sin). A lord of the manor can count on the annual *chevage* from each of his villeins. If you are the younger child of a king or prince, your father will have of course arranged for a suitable *appanage* to support you. Less elevated persons also had their incomes. British officers in India could at one time count on their *batta*, or extra pay for serving there, and the Lord Mayor's butler and yeoman of the cellar could look forward to their *cellarage*, money collected from the attendees at a Lord Mayor's feast.

Unfortunately, these suggestions for increasing your wealth are probably not very valuable. If they leave you with *nuppence* ('no money'), you could say that they are not worth a *rig-marie*, a *scuddick*, a *sharpshin*, a *skilligalee*, or a (brass) *razoo*—all words meaning 'a coin of very little value' and equivalent to that equally worthless *red cent*.

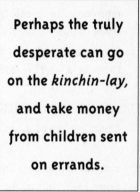

morioplasty [**mor**-ee-oh-plas-tee] the restoration of lost parts of the body. Obviously, this word is used in a surgical context, but the mental picture of two policemen at the door, asking, "Sir, is this your leg?" is a pleasant one.

morology [muh-**rah**-luh-djee] foolish talking, also, humorously, the study of fools. From a Greek word of the same meaning. A related word is *moromancy*, glossed as 'foolish divination,' but more useful as a word to mean 'telling the future by observing the behavior of fools.'

motatorious [moh-tuh-**tor**-ee-us] in constant motion. Usually used about the legs of insects, a revolting concept.

mouche [moosh] a small patch of beard grown under the lower lip. From Latin *musca*, 'fly.'

Mountweazel [**mownt**-wee-zul] a fake word or name invented by reference-book editors to trap plagiarists. It comes from Lillian Virginia Mountweazel, whose (fake) entry in an edition of the *New Columbia Encyclopedia* was a triumph of the form. ("Mountweazel" died in an explosion while on assignment for *Combustibles* magazine.)

mournival [**mor**-ni-vul] a set of four kings, queens, jacks, or aces in one hand, or any set of four things or people. This comes from a French word whose literal meaning is 'a slap in the face.'

mouton enrage [moo-tahn-ahn-rah-**zhay**] literally, 'mad sheep.' A term for an angry person who is usually calm.

mucronate [**myoo**-kruh-nate] an adjective meaning 'coming to a hard sharp point.' The pencils of the truly detail-oriented can be described as mucronate.

muculency [**myoo**-kyuh-lun-see] an obsolete word meaning 'snottiness.'

mulciberian [mull-suh-**beer**-ee-un] an adjective meaning 'resembling Vulcan.' Originally meaning the mythological figure, but ripe to be picked up by fervent Trekkers.

muliebrity [myoo-lee-**eb**-ri-tee] womanly qualities or womanliness. The term comes from the Latin word for woman: unlike its masculine counterpart *virility* (from the Latin for 'man'), it is rarely used except in formal or literary writing.

multatitious [mull-tuh-**tish**-us] a rare word meaning 'acquired by fine or forfeit.' In certain localities the local police can confiscate cars and other property used in the commission of a crime; this word might be useful to them.

mundation [muhn-**day**-shuhn] the action of cleaning or the state of being clean. From a Latin word meaning 'clean.'

mundungus [muhn-**dung**-guhs] a rare word meaning 'bad-smelling tobacco.' It comes from a humorous use of a Spanish word meaning 'tripe.'

murenger [**myoor**-in-djer] an obsolete word meaning 'an officer who is responsible for keeping the walls of a city in good condition.'

murgeon [**mur**-djun] a plural noun meaning 'grimaces.' Its origin is obscure.

musophobist [myoo-**zah**-fuh-bist] a person who regards poetry with suspicious dislike. From Greek words meaning 'muse' and 'fear.' This word was used (and probably coined) by the poet Algernon Charles Swinburne (1837–1909), who quite possibly inspired more than a few *musophobes*.

mussitation [mus-i-**tay**-shuhn] muttering, murmuring. From a Latin word with the same meaning.

mutuatitial [myoo-choo-uh-**tish**-ul] an obsolete and rare adjective meaning 'borrowed.' As a noun it means 'something borrowed.' The verb form is *mutuate*. They come from a Latin word meaning 'borrow.'

mycterism [**mick**-tuh-riz-um] a rare word meaning 'a taunt or sneer,' from a Greek root meaning 'nose' (that being what you sneer with).

myomancy [**mye**-uh-man-see] divination by the movements of mice. Modern scientists probably study the movements of mice as much or more as the ancient *myomancers* ever did, and for ends that are not dissimilar.

MYOMANCY

nabocklish [na-**bock**-lish] an incredibly useful Irish interjection meaning 'Never mind! Leave that alone!' Literally meaning 'don't meddle with it.'

nacket [**nack**-it] a rude and impertinent boy. From French words meaning 'the tennis court keeper's boy.' Another *nacket*, of obscure origin, means 'a light lunch, a snack.' The two words should be easy to keep straight, unless you're a cannibal, in which case there is a pleasant congruence.

naevose [**nee**-vose] a rare adjective meaning 'spotted, freckled.' A *naevus* is a raised red or purple birthmark caused by hypertrophied blood vessels in the skin. The US spelling is *nevus*.

nanism [**nay**-niz-um] the condition of being dwarfed, or the tendency to become stunted or dwarfed. Usually used about animals and plants. *Nanity* is the condition of having any abnormal deficiency. Both words come from a Greek word meaning 'dwarf.'

nannicock [**nann**-ee-kock] an obsolete and rare word, so obsolete and rare the *OED* just notes its existence and does not give any meaning for it. The one citation is from 1600: "Hee that doth wonder at a Weathercocke . . . And is in loue with euery *Nannicocke*." Since there is no accepted meaning, please feel free to go forth and use it in any (mildly disparaging) sense you like.

naology [nay-**ah**-luh-djee] the study of churches, temples, and other sacred buildings. *Naometry* is the measurement of sacred buildings. From a Greek word meaning 'temple.'

naufragate [**naw**-fri-gate] an obsolete and rare verb meaning 'to wreck.' If something is *naufrageous*, it is in danger of shipwreck; if it is *naufragous*, it causes shipwreck. These all derive from a Latin word meaning 'to suffer shipwreck.'

nauscopy [**naw**-skuh-pee] the art of seeing the approach of ships or landfall from a considerable distance. The *OED* goes on to say "This pretended art was invented by a M. Bottineau . . . from the year 1782 to 1784." Bottineau claimed that he could see past the horizon by observing the effects that approaching ships had on the atmosphere. The governor of Mauritius requested that he keep a record of his predictions, and he successfully predicted the arrival of more than 550 ships, some as many as four days before they arrived. He turned down an offer of 3,000 francs for his secret and died in 1789.

nazar [**naz**-ahr] in India, a present made to a superior by an inferior, especially one made upon being introduced.

neoplorgismanteau [**nee**-oh-**plorg**-is-**man**-toh] a word meaning 'a new word (*neologism*) formed by putting together two existing words (*portmanteau*).' As such, *neoplorgismanteau* is a neoplorgismanteau. The word seems to have been coined by Wikipedia user BDAbramson, who put up a humorous article about his creation on the site.

neoteny [nee-**ah**-tuh-nee] the preservation of juvenile characteristics well into maturity, especially where these characteristics are attractive. This word comes from Greek roots meaning 'extend' and 'young.'

nexility [nek-**sil**-i-tee] speed or pithiness of speech. (This entry deliberately left short as an example.)

nidgery [**nij**-uh-ree] an obsolete adjective meaning 'trifling, fidgety, foppish.' It comes from a (now also obsolete) French word meaning the same thing.

nidor [**nye**-der] the smell of burning fat, or any strong meat-cooking smell. It has been applied, unfortunately, to the smell of burning martyred flesh: "The nidor of a human creature roasted for faith."

nidulation [nidj-oo-**lay**-shun] nesting or nest making. Also, *nidification*. A *nidifugous* bird is a bird that has young that are able to leave the nest immediately after birth. These words all come from a Latin word meaning 'nest.'

niefling [**neef**-ling] a nongendered word meaning 'a niece or nephew,' useful as shorthand, e.g., "I promised my sister that I'd watch my nieflings this Saturday." This word was coined by Susan Parker Martin of New York.

nighwhat [**nye**-(h)waht] an obsolete adverb meaning 'nearly, almost.' Perhaps because it's obsolete, it sounds very hillbillyish to modern ears: "He was nighwhat kilt when that there hog jumped onto his truck!"

nihilarian [nye-(h)il-**air**-ee-uhn] a person who deals with things of no importance (whether by choice or not is unclear). Formed from the Latin root *nihil*-, meaning 'nothing,' on the example of *unitarian*, etc.

nim [nim] a game in which two players take one or more counters from any one of several piles, the goal being to force one's opponent to take the last counter (or sometimes, to take it oneself). This word may come either from another *nim*, meaning 'thief,' or perhaps from the German word *nehmen*, meaning 'to take.'

nimfadoro [nim-fuh-**dor**-oh] an effeminate fellow, especially one who is well dressed and popular with women. The example in the *OED*, a quote from the playwright Ben Jonson, talks about the *nimfadoro* wearing 'white virgin boot[s].'

nimptopsical [nim-**tops**-ih-kul] drunk. This word is one of more than 200 synonyms for 'drunk' compiled by Benjamin Franklin; some of the others included *cherry-merry, lappy,* and "been too free with Sir Richard."

ninguid [**ning**-gwid] an adjective meaning 'having much snow,' used to describe a place. From a Latin word *ninguis*, meaning 'snow.'

nippitate [**nip**-i-tate] an obscure word meaning 'good strong ale.' The word is sometimes found with faux-Latin endings, such as *nippitatum* and *nippitati*.

nithing [**nye**-thing] an archaic word for a contemptible or despicable person. It arose in the second half of the tenth century from Old Norse, and it later developed the additional meaning of 'a mean or miserly person.'

nittiness [**nit**-ee-nis] an obsolete word meaning 'the condition of being full of small air bubbles.' The one citation in the *OED* seems to be about wine.

niveous [**niv**-ee-us] an adjective meaning 'snowy' or 'resembling snow.' A word used mainly in literary writing, it comes from the Latin word for snow.

Nobodaddy [**noh**-boh-dad-ee] a word used by William Blake as a disrespectful name for God. By extension, used for someone no longer admired. A blend of *nobody* and *daddy*.

nocency [**noh**-sun-see] an obsolete word meaning 'guilt.' This is the thing than *innocence* is the opposite of. Something that is *nocent* is harmful or criminal.

noceur [**naw**-sur] someone who stays up late at night. Also, 'a rake or libertine.' Rakes and libertines are hardly ever in their beds before ten. (Someone else's bed, sure, but not their own.) From a French word of the same meaning.

noctograph [**nock**-toh-graf] a tool for writing used by a blind person. The *noctograph* seems to have used an early form of carbon paper, with wires to guide the pen or stylus of the writer. The word also means 'a device or log to track the progress of night watchmen or guards on their rounds.' From Latin words meaning 'night' and 'writing.'

nod-crafty [**nahd**-kraf-tee] an adjective meaning 'able to nod with an air of great wisdom.' An essential characteristic of college professors and television talking heads and presenters.

nomothete [**nah**-muh-theet] a rare word meaning 'a lawgiver or legislator.' *Nomo-* is a Greek root meaning 'law.' Other *nomo-* words include *nomography*, 'the expression of law in written form,' *nomology*, 'the inductive science of law' or 'the science of the conformity of action to rules,' and *nomocracy*, 'government based on a legal code.'

notarikon [noh-**tarr**-i-kun] a word from kabbala, meaning 'the art of making a new word from the letters taken from the beginning (or middle, or end) of the words in a sentence.' A Greekification of a Latin word meaning 'shorthand writer.'

nudiustertian [n(y)oo-dee-uh-**stur**-shun] an obsolete and rare (yet incredibly useful) word meaning 'of the day before yesterday.' Used by extension also to mean 'the very newest.' From a Latin phrase meaning 'three days earlier.'

nullibicity [null-uh-**biss**-i-tee] a rare word meaning 'the condition of not existing anywhere.' The adjective is *nullibiquitous*. The *nullibicity* of certain information on the Internet continues to surprise and amaze many people, who assume that everything has been put up on the Web, somewhere. A *nullibist* is a person who believes that a spirit or incorporeal being does not exist. From a Latin word meaning 'nowhere.'

SEX IN THE NULLIBICITY

nullo [**null**-oh] someone who has undergone an elective amputation for the purposes of body modification, usually of a toe, but sometimes of a hand or limb.

nundination [nun-di-**nay**-shuhn] buying and selling, trade. From the Latin word *nundine*, a market-day held every eight (by Roman counting, nine) days.

nychthemeral [nik-**them**-er-uhl] an adjective that means 'occurring with a variation that matches night and day.' It comes from a Greek word meaning 'lasting for a day and a night.' A *nychthemeron* is a period of twenty-four hours. These words are fairly rare, but one can imagine their use quite easily: "'Not one *nychthemeron* more shall I tarry,' cried the heroine," or "They complained about the *nychthemeral* variation in traffic outside of the Hamptons' hottest nightspot."

nyctophobia [nik-tuh-**foh**-bee-uh] extreme or irrational fear of the night or of darkness. It comes from the Greek word for night: a related word in English is *nyctalopia*, the term for a medical condition characterized by the inability to see at night or in dim light.

obacerate [oh-**bass**-uh-rate] an obsolete and rare word meaning 'to contradict.' *Obaceration* is the action of shutting someone's mouth— whether metaphorically or physically is not clear.

obambulate [ob-**am**-byuh-late] a rare word meaning 'to walk about, wander.' *Obambulatory* is the adjective, meaning 'habitually walking around.' Most of the citations in the *OED* seem to refer to ghosts and spirits. From a Latin word meaning 'to walk.'

obliquangled [o-blee-**kang**-guld] an obsolete form (but wonderful to say) of *oblique-angled*. A good figurative use would be to extend this word to mean 'messy, awkward': "I tried to put it together but it got all *obliquangled*."

obuncous [oh-**bunk**-us] a rare and obsolete words meaning 'very crooked.' Useful for describing politicans whose graft is worthy of extraordinary comment.

ochlesis [ahk-**lee**-sis] a disease caused by overcrowding, especially in a hospital. This would be a good word for the inevitable cold that arises from air travel.

ochlophobia [ahk-luh-**foh**-bee-uh] extreme or irrational fear of or aversion to crowds. A rare term, it comes from a Greek word meaning 'crowd' or 'mob.'

octothorpe [**ahk**-tuh-thorp] the telephone keypad symbol '#'; also called *pound, number sign, hash,* or *crosshatch.* This key and the '*' (*asterisk*) key were introduced by Bell Laboratories in the early 1960s on the then-new touch-tone telephones. Don MacPherson, a Bell Labs engineer, coined the word from *octo-* (for the eight points) and *Thorpe* (Mr. MacPherson was active in an organization lobbying for the return of Jim Thorpe's Olympic medals. His medals were taken away after it was revealed that he was not strictly an amateur, having been paid for playing baseball when he was a youth. The medals were posthumously restored in 1982).

oggannition [ah-guh-**ni**-shuhn] an obsolete and rare word meaning 'snarling, growling.' From a Latin word meaning 'yelp or growl at.'

oligosyllable [ah-li-guh-**si**-luh-buhl] a word of fewer than four syllables. *Oligo-* comes from a Greek root meaning 'small, little, few.'

Ollendorffian [ah-lun-**dorf**-ee-un] an adjective meaning 'written in the artificial and overly formal style of foreign-language phrase books.' From the name of Heinrich Gottfried Ollendorff (1803–1865), a German grammarian and educator. Famous examples of such language include "Stop, the postilion has been struck by lightning!", "A man is drowning. Is there a life buoy, a rope, a grapnel at hand?", and "Unhand me Sir, for my husband, who is an Australian, awaits without." (Which last deserves several readings at different levels.) Perhaps the most absurd phrasebook is *English as She is Spoke: The new guide of the conversation in Portuguese and English in two parts* (1855), by Pedro Caroline and Jose da Fonseca, which includes this nearly incomprehensible sentence in its introduction: "We expect then, who the little book (for the care what we wrote him, and for her typographical correction) that may be worth the expectation of the studious persons, and especially of the Youth, at which we dedicate him particularly."

IMPLUVIOUS OMBRIFUGE

ombrifuge [**ahm**-bruh-fyoodj] a rare word meaning 'a rain shelter.'
From a Greek word meaning 'a shower of rain.' A semantically related
word is *paravent*, 'a wind shelter.'

omnifarious [ahm-ni-**fair**-ee-us] an adjective meaning 'dealing with all kinds of things' or 'of all kinds or forms.'

omophagy [oh-**mah**-fuh-jee] the eating of raw food, especially raw meat. The word was originally used in reference to feasts for the Greek god Bacchus, at which raw flesh was eaten. It comes from the Greek for 'raw.'

omphaloskeptic [ahm-fuh-loh-**skep**-tik] a person who indulges in navel-gazing; that is, someone who is self-absorbed. Unless, of course, one means the *omphalopsychites*, who engaged in navel-gazing as a means of bringing on a hypnotic reverie. *Omphalo-* comes from a Greek word meaning 'navel.' Another fun *omphalo-* word is *omphalomancy*, which is the practice of predicting the number of future children of a mother by counting the knots in the first child's umbilical cord.

oneirocritical [oh-nye-roh-**krit**-i-cle] an adjective meaning 'expert in the interpretation of dreams.'

onolatry [oh-**nah**-luh-tree] a very rare word meaning 'the worship of donkeys or asses.' It is taken from a Greek word meaning 'ass,' and another word based on this root is *onocentaur*, a term from Greek mythology that refers to a centaur with the body of an ass rather than that of a horse.

ooglification [oog-li-fi-**cay**-shuhn] the substitution of an "OO" sound for another vowel sound to make a standard English word into a slang word or to make a slang word even slangier. *Cigaroot* for *cigarette* is a good example of *ooglification*. We may not be seeing *phoot* for *phat* any time soon, though. This was coined by Roger W. Wescott, in "Ooglification in American English Slang," *VERBATIM* III, 4 (1977).

opsimath [**ahp**-si-math] a person who begins to learn or study late in life. A rare term, it comes from Greek words meaning 'late' and 'to learn.' A related word in English is *polymath*, a person with a very wide range of knowledge.

opsophagize [ahp-**sah**-fuh-jize] to eat delicacies, especially fish. *Opsophagist* is the agent noun. From a Greek word of the same meaning.

oredelf [**or**-delf] the right to dig minerals; the digging of ore. An obsolete legal term, this comes from *ore* plus the word *delf*, meaning 'mine, digging.' *Delf* is related to *ditch*.

orexigenic [o-**rex**-i-jen-ik] causing appetite, or related to the stimulation of appetite. It's used mostly for food, but it could be a useful word to describe effective advertising.

orgulous [**or**-gyoo-luhs] an adjective meaning 'proud' or 'haughty,' found chiefly in very literary writing. It dates from Middle English, and there is almost no evidence of its use after the sixteenth century until the writers Robert Southey (1774–1843) and Walter Scott (1771–1832) began to employ it as a historical archaism in the early 1800s.

oryctognosy [or-ick-**tog**-nuh-see] an obsolete word meaning 'knowledge of minerals.' From Greek words meaning 'dug up' and 'knowledge.'

oryzivorous [or-i-**ziv**-er-us] an adjective meaning 'rice eating.' As in "I used to be *oryzivorous*, but now I'm on that high-protein diet."

osphresiology [ahs-free-see-**ah**-luh-djee] the study of the sense of smell, or a scientific paper about smelling and scents. From a Greek word meaning 'smell.'

ostentiferous [ahs-tun-**tiff**-er-us] an obsolete and rare word meaning 'that which brings monsters or strange sights.' An *ostent* is a 'a sign or wonder, a portent.' From a Latin word meaning 'something shown.'

ostrobogulous [ahs-truh-**bahg**-yoo-luhs] a word used for something indecent or slightly risqué, or anything 'bizarre, unusual, or interesting.' This word is associated with the writer Victor B. Neuberg (1883–1940), who gave it the etymology 'full of (from Latin *ulus*) rich (from Greek *ostro*) dirt (schoolboy *bog*).' Related words include *ostrobogulatory*, *ostrobogulation*, and *ostrobogulosity*.

otacust [**oh**-tuh-kust] an obsolete word meaning 'eavesdropper, spy.' From Greek roots meaning 'ear' and 'listener.'

otenchyte [**oht**-n-kite] a tool or device for injecting liquid into the ears. Presumably for medicinal purposes, but it also sounds suitable as one of those "ways of making you talk." From Greek words meaning 'ear' and 'pour in.'

ouche [owch] a word, now only in poetic use, for a jeweled clasp used to keep two sides of a garment together. Even though it looks like *ouch* and actually has a sense 'wound,' it's not related.

oultrepreu [oo-truh-**proo**] an obsolete and rare word meaning 'very brave.' From a French word meaning 'beyond brave.'

oxter [**ahks**-ter] a Scottish and northern English word for a person's armpit. It comes from Old English.

pactitious [pack-**tish**-us] an obsolete and rare adjective meaning 'characterized by being agreed upon or specified in a contract.'

paddereen [pad-er-**reen**] an Irish word meaning 'a bead of the rosary,' and, figuratively, 'a bullet.' From a diminutive form of a word meaning 'the Lord's Prayer.'

palang [puh-**lang**] the practice, originating in Borneo, of piercing the penis with a gold or tin bolt. In the middle of the bolt is a hole to allow for urination. This practice is said to have persisted in Borneo until at least 1974, and it is occasionally done in the United States today as elective body modification.

palestral [puh-**les**-truhl] an adjective meaning 'pertaining to wrestling' (and by extension, to athletics in general). From a Greek word meaning 'to wrestle.'

pampination [pam-pi-**nay**-shuhn] the trimming of vines. From a Latin word meaning 'vine-shoot.'

pandiculation [pan-di-kyoo-**lay**-shuhn] the stretching of the body that often accompanies yawning. This word is also sometimes used to mean yawning itself. It comes from a Latin word meaning 'to stretch oneself.'

panmixis [pan-**mik**-sis] a population in which random mating takes place. Mostly applied to animals but equally well suited to any large city or college campus.

pannage [**pan**-ij] the right to pasture pigs in a wood, or the payment for that right. This might be useful to revive as a modern word for dog-walking privileges in a yard or common area, and it might encourage pet owners to apply for (and pay for) such rights.

panthnetist [pan-**thnee**-tist] someone who believes that both the body and soul perish in death. From Greek roots meaning 'all' and 'mortal.'

panyarring [puh-**nyar**-ing] the act of kidnapping someone into slavery. The verb is *panyar*. It comes from a Latin word meaning 'pawn.' It was mostly used in West Africa.

papabili [puh-**pah**-buh-lee] in the Roman Catholic church, the likely candidates for being elected Pope. Now often used of contenders for any high office.

paradiorthosis [parr-uh-dye-or-**thoh**-sis] an obsolete and rare word meaning 'a false correction.' Unfortunately, the practice of introducing errors into text that is already just fine is not as rare as this word.

parataxic [parr-uh-**tack**-sick] a term used by the psychologist H. S. Sullivan (1892–1949) to describe the condition in which subconscious attitudes or emotions affect relationships. A *parataxic distortion* is when you attribute traits of significant people in your past to people with whom you currently have a relationship. The opposite of *parataxis* is *syntaxis*, in which happy state objectivity and the use of "consensually validated symbols" (in other words, things that both people agree upon the meaning of) are the basis for communication.

parergon [puh-**rer**-gahn] secondary work or business, separate from one's main work or ordinary employment. A handy (and cloaking) synonym for *moonlighting*. From Greek roots meaning 'beside' and 'work.'

pareschatology [perr-es-kuh-**tah**-luh-jee] the name given to theories about life after physical death but before the final (Christian) resurrection. The word comes from a Greek word meaning 'study of next to last things' (the last thing being resurrection). *Eschatology* is the study of last things.

parorexia [parr-uh-**reck**-see-uh] an unnatural appetite, or an unnatural lack of appetite. A near synonym for *anorexia*.

pasquinade [pas-kwi-**nade**] a satirical piece of writing posted in a public place. *Pasquin* was the name of a statue in Rome that was often dressed up to resemble a mythological or historical figure on St. Mark's Day (April 25th). Students often composed verses to salute Pasquin on his big day, and the verses were written on or posted by the statue. The verses soon became satirical and the custom spread to other countries, where satirical writings (with or without the benefit of convenient statues to rest upon) were often signed "Pasquin."

PECULIAR AND
PREOCCUPYING PASTIMES

If you're bored with hide-and-seek, Go Fish, or *Doom*, you might want to try some of these entertaingly named games. Perhaps *able-whackets*, a card game where (according to the *OED*, quoting Smyth's *Sailor's Word-book*) the loser "is beaten over the palms of the hands with a handkerchief tightly twisted like a rope. Very popular with horny-fisted sailors." You could try *rythmomachy*, also called *the philosophers' game*, played with round, triangular, and square pieces, each marked with a number, on a board like two chessboards joined together. Robert Burton considered it a cure for melancholy.

If that sounds too much like work, there's always *cottabus*, an ancient Greek drinking game in which the goal was to throw wine from your cup into another container in a particular way (which seems the opposite of modern drinking games, in which the object is to get wine from your cup into you).

Many boy-and-girl games are defined in the *OED*, including *course-a-park*, a country game where a girl calls out a boy's name for him to chase her. (It's assumed that she doesn't try too hard not to be caught.) There's also *draw-glove*, where players race to take off their gloves (back when men and women wore gloves) at the mention of certain words. Winners tended to be awarded kisses. If, at a party, a double nut (called a *fillipeen*) was found by a lady, she gave one of the kernels to a gentleman to eat. Then, when they met again, each person tried to be the first to say "*Fillipeen!*" because the first one to say it was entitled to a present from the other.

Other games are more physical and less flirty. *Bumdockdousse* (also called *pimpompet*) is a game where you try to hit the other players on their rear ends with your feet. In *hinch-pinch,* one person hits another softly, the other player hits back with a little more force, and each subsequent blow in turn is harder, until it becomes a real fight. *Bumble-puppy* is essentially tetherball with a racket (but a *bumblepuppist* is someone who plays unscientific whist).

Kabaddi is a kind of pushing game popular in northern India and Pakistan, in which players have to hold their breath during their turns. (They prove this by saying "kabaddi" over and over again.) *Knappan* is an old Welsh game in which each side tries to drive a wooden ball as far as possible in one direction. One wonders if there was any practical limit on the distance, or if a very powerful team could find themselves miles from home at the end of the game!

> ***Bumble-puppy* is essentially tetherball with a racket (but a *bumblepuppist* is someone who plays unscientific whist).**

Many games are underdefined or undefined, so that their object or goal is obscure. *Bubble-the-justice* is a 'game of nine holes.' *Warpling o' the green* is defined as 'a rustic game' (and sounds suspiciously like something out of *Cold Comfort Farm*). *Dingthrift, gresco, prelleds, penneech, rowland-hoe, sitisot,* and *whipperginnie* are all just defined with variants of "some game." It's a shame to have such good game-names go unused—feel free to make up your own rules and ludically reclaim them.

passiuncle [pas-ee-**ung**-k'l] a petty or contemptible passion. This is a nonce-word that deserves a wider field. "He has a *passiuncle* for Ring Dings." Formed from the word *passion* with the diminutive ending -*uncle*, like that of *vibratiuncle*, 'a slight vibration.'

pathognomy [path-**ahg**-nuh-mee] the study of the emotions, or the physical signs or expressions of them. A nice word that could possibly be extended to mean 'the study of tantrums.'

patteroller [pat-uh-**roll**-er] a person who watches over slaves at night. From *patroller*, and mostly used in the pre–Civil War South.

pavisande [**pav**-uh-sand] to flaunt opulent or expensive clothing or jewels; an Edwardian synonym for *bling*. It might be related to *pavisade*, a screen or canvas erected around a ship to protect the crew.

pechnidiocrisia [petch-nid-ee-oh-**kris**-yah] criticism or censorship of video games.

pedionomite [pe-dee-**ah**-nuh-mite] a person who lives on a plain. From a Greek word meaning 'plain-dweller.'

pedotrophy [pee-**dah**-truh-fee] the bringing up or raising of children. The British spelling is *paedotrophy*. A particularly good mother or father could be described as a *pedotrophist*. However, given the general tenor and the recent trends in memoir, if this word finds a new popularity, it is sure to be in the negative: "My parents were by no means *pedotrophists*."

NIDIFUGOUS PEENGERS

peenge [peendj] to complain in a whining voice. One suspects that the qualification "in a whining voice" is unnecessary. Perhaps formed from *whinge*, and influenced by *peevish*.

peirastic [pye-**ras**-tik] an adjective meaning 'tentative, experimental.' From a Greek word meaning 'of the nature of trying.'

pelmatogram [pel-**mat**-uh-gram] a high-flown word meaning 'foot-print.' From a Greek word meaning 'sole of the foot.'

pelotherapy [pee-loh-**therr**-uh-pee] medicinal mud baths or treatments. If these help you, you might be *pelophilous* ('mud-loving'). From a Greek word meaning 'mud.'

peplos [**pep**-lahs] a shawl worn by women in ancient Greece, especially a ceremonial one woven yearly for the statue of Athena at Athens, which was embroidered with mythological subjects and carried in procession to her temple.

peramene [perr-uh-**meen**] an obsolete and rare adjective meaning 'very pleasant.'

percoarcted [per-koh-**ark**-tid] an obsolete and rare word meaning 'brought into a narrow room,' useful for anyone who has ever had to move a large piece of furniture. *Coarct* is an obsolete verb meaning 'kept within narrow limits, restricted.'

percontation [per-kahn-**tay**-shun] a rare word meaning 'an inquiry.' The adjective is *percontatorial*, meaning 'inquisitive.' From a Latin word meaning 'to interrogate.'

percribrate [per-**krib**-rate] an obsolete and rare word meaning 'to sift.' From a Latin word meaning 'to sift thoroughly.' One of the citations in the *OED*, from 1668, is "Thy Brain thus blown up by the *percribrated* influence of thy moist Mistress, the Moon." Which, even sifted a few times, makes little sense out of context, and possibly not much more in context. This proves that even nonsense can be good enough to show the meaning of a word.

perculsion [per-**kull**-shun] a rare word meaning 'a severe shock, consternation.' From a Latin word meaning 'to upset.' Something that is *perculsive* gives you a shock.

percunctorily [per-**kungk**-ter-uh-lee] an obsolete word meaning 'lazily.' From a Latin word meaning 'to loiter,' on the model of *perfunctorily*.

perhendinancer [per-**hen**-duh-nun-ser] a rare and obsolete word meaning 'a lodger, a traveler.' From a Latin word that literally means 'to defer until the day after tomorrow.'

perissology [pe-ri-**sah**-luh-jee] an obsolete rhetorical term meaning 'redundancy of speech, pleonasm.' From a Greek word meaning 'speaking too much.'

pertainym [per-**tay**-nim] a name for an adjective that is usually defined with the phrase "of or pertaining to." *Abdominal, friarish,* and *heraldic* are all *pertainyms. Pertainyms* do not have antonyms. From *pertain* and the suffix *-nym,* meaning 'word.'

petrichor [**pet**-rih-kor] the pleasant smell that sometimes accompanies rain, especially the first rain after a period of warm dry weather.

phenakism [**fen**-uh-kiz-um] a rare word meaning 'cheating, trickery.' From a Greek word meaning 'deception.'

phenology [fi-**nah**-luh-jee] the study of the timing of recurring natural phenomena, such as volcanic explosion, rainfall and temperature variation, or the flowering times of plants. This word is an anglicization of a German word with the same meaning, taking the parts *pheno-* (as in phenomenon) and *-logical* (as in meteorological).

philobat [**fil**-uh-bat] a person who enjoys coping with dangerous situations, preferably alone. The first citation in the *OED*, from Michael Balint in 1955, reads "Greek scholars among my readers will know that 'acrobat' means literally 'one who walks on his toes,' i.e. away from the safe earth. Taking this word as my model I shall use 'philobat' to describe one who enjoys such thrills." A person who avoids dangerous situations and clings to others for safety is an *ocnophil*. *Ocnophil* comes from a Greek word meaning 'to hesitate.'

philocomal [fi-**lah**-koh-mul] an adjective meaning 'characterized by love of or attention to the hair.'

philostorgy [**fi**-luh-stor-jee] natural affection, such as that between parents and children. From a Greek word meaning 'tenderly loving.'

phobanthropy [fah-**ban**-thruh-pee] the 'morbid dread of mankind.' From Greek words meaning 'fear' and 'man,' influenced by *philanthropy*.

phoenicurous [fen-i-**kyoor**-us] an adjective that unfortunately does not mean 'taking care of phoenixes.' It means 'having a red tail.' From a Greek word meaning 'red-tailed.'

phonascetics [foh-nuh-**set**-iks] a rare word for a kind of treatment for improving or strengthening the voice. From a Greek word meaning 'one who exercises the voice.'

phonendoscope [foh-**nen**-duh-scope] an instrument for amplifying small sounds of the human body, or within other solid bodies. Just in case you thought your stomach growling wasn't loud enough, you can use your handy *phonendoscope* and make sure the whole room hears. From Greek words meaning 'voice' and 'within.'

phonocamptics [foh-noh-**kamp**-ticks] the part of acoustics that deals with reflected sounds or echoes. From *phono-* plus a Greek word meaning 'to bend.'

photuria [foh-**t(y)oo**-ree-uh] phosphorescence of the urine. From Greek roots meaning 'light' and 'urine,' but the real question is, how does this happen and how does one happen to find this out?

physitheism [fi-zi-**thee**-i-zum] the deification of the weather. From Greek words meaning 'nature' and 'God.'

piacular [pye-**ak**-yoo-luhr] a rare adjective meaning 'making or requiring atonement.' It comes from a Latin verb meaning 'to appease,' as does *expiate*, which means to atone or to make amends for one's wrongdoing.

pilgarlic [pil-**gahr**-lik] a bald person, or a person who is held in humorous contempt or treated with mock pity. The word means 'peeled garlic.'

PECULIAR AND
PRODIGIOUS PIGS

Although theology and science seem to have more than their fair share of weird words, the most mundane things can often be described by unusual words. The *gussie* or *grunting-cheat* ('pig') is quite possibly the most mundane of animals, but is described by many fascinating *suillary* ('of swine') or *aprine* ('of wild swine') terms.

The pig's snout, that icon of piggishness, is a *rowel*. With it, a pig can *whick* or *wrine* 'squeal' or *grout* 'turn up the ground.' Of course, a pig can also *moil* 'wallow' in the mud.

A pig-sty is a *cruive* or *piggery*. A woodland pasture for pigs is a *drove-den* or *denn*. Pigswill (or *mingle-mangle*) is *draff*, especially if it's from a brewery; it's eaten in a *stug*, or pig-trough. Nuts, especially acorns, used as food for pigs are called *mast*. When a pig has eaten a lot of *mast*, it's called *mastiff* or *masty* 'fat.'

A pig less than a year old is a *sheat*. A young weaned pig is a *shoat, speaning*, or *spaneling*. A young pig is also a *bonham*, a *boneen*, a *snork*, a *farrow*, a *gruntling*, a *grice*, or a *griceling*. A young sow is a *gilt*. A boar less than two years old is a *sounder* or *hogget*. There are, not surprisingly, no terms for an old pig; pigs don't live to be old. They live to be bacon.

The smallest pig in the litter, the runt, is also called the *whinnock, tit-man, croot, reckling, wrig, rit, wreckling, wregling*, or *ritling*. A pig in heat is *brim*, and quite possibly *breme* 'fierce.'

A suckling pig baked whole in a pie is called *mermaid-pie*. If the pig is stuffed with forcemeat first, it's *enfarced*. If you're still hungry, *charlet* is a kind of custard of milk, eggs, and pork, and *smotheration* is a sailor's meal of beef and pork covered with potatoes. A dangerous-sounding pork dish is *Polony sausage*, which is served partially cooked. Small cakes of pork combined with lots of other ingredients (which remain unspecified) are called (or were called, the word is archaic) *raynolls*. Fat pork meat is called *speck*, especially in the United States and South Africa, and if pigs are scarce the word can also be applied to the fat of a hippopotamus. But not, if you're kind, where the hippopotamus can overhear. Pork is

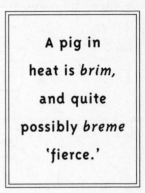

A pig in heat is *brim,* and quite possibly *breme* 'fierce.'

also called *grunting-peck* or *grice*, and the lean part of the pig's loin is called *griskin*. A pig's hoof is a *cloot;* when it's cooked it's a *crubeen* or *pettitoes*, when pickled, *souse*. The ham or haunch of a pig, especially when eaten fresh, is called a *pestle*.

A common Scots proper name for a pig is *Grumphie* (used much the same way as *Spot* is for a dog). The *piggard* is set to watch Grumphie and the other pigs, and he rules in *pigdom*, the realm of pigs. If he does his job well, he's certain to end up a *piggicide*. If he's fat like a pig, he's a *porknell*, all the better to make him *long-pig:* human flesh from the cannibal's point of view.

pilliver [**pi**-li-ver] a pillowcase. From Old English words meaning 'pillow' and 'cover.' Another, more archaic synonym is *pillow-bere*.

pinguescence [ping-**gwes**-uhns] a rare word for the process of growing fat. It's also used loosely to mean obesity.

pinjrapol [**pinj**-ruh-pohl] in India, a pen or enclosure where sick or old animals are kept.

piscation [pis-**kay**-shuhn] a rare word for fishing. A related term in English is *piscatorial*, meaning 'having to do with fishermen or fishing'; this is found mainly in formal writing, although it may also be used for humorous effect.

pishachi [pi-**shah**-chee] a female devil or ghost, especially one that dislikes travelers and pregnant women.

planeticose [pluh-**nee**-ti-kohs] an adjective meaning 'liking to wander.' *Planet* comes from a Greek word meaning 'wanderer.'

plenisphere [**plen**-i-sfeer] a perfect sphere. From a Latin word meaning 'full,' plus *sphere*.

pleonexia [plee-uh-**neck**-see-uh] greediness or avarice as a mental illness. From a Greek word meaning 'greed.' A similar adjective is *lucripetous*, 'eager for gain,' which comes from a Latin word meaning 'to seek gain.'

plethysmograph [pli-**thiz**-muh-graff] an instrument that measures the changes in volume of a part of the body, especially changes in blood flow such as those caused by emotion. A citation from 1882 claims that "the *plethysmograph* . . . measures the amount of blood sent to the brain in any particular process of thought, and records the exact time for each process." It seems as if in the early days this was very uncomfortable, as the *plethysmograph* was described as "a rigid airtight container enclosing the subject entirely except for [the] head and neck."

plevisable [**plev**-iss-uh-bul] an obsolete law term meaning 'able to be bailed out.' From a French word meaning 'to warrant.'

plew [ploo] a beaver skin. In former times, the skin of a beaver was used in Canada as a standard unit of value in the fur trade: the word comes from a Canadian French adjective meaning 'hairy.'

ploddeill [plah-**deal**] a rare and obsolete word meaning 'a band of cudgellers.' (The *OED* marks this word as 'contemptuous,' although I don't know how contemptuous the average dictionary editor would be if faced with a band of men carrying cudgels.)

plongeur [plahn-**zhoor**] a superior word for a dishwasher in a hotel or restaurant. The *OED* has this citation from the *Daily Telegraph*, from 1977: "Titles are nice but surely the Dorchester is going a little too far advertising for a 'Supervisor Plongeur' to head the washing up department."

pluteus [**ploo**-tee-uhs] a shelf for books, small statues, etc. This comes from an identically spelled Latin word that originally meant 'a barrier or light wall between columns.'

pluviculture [**ploo**-vi-kul-chur] the science of making rain, or schemes for inducing rain. From a Latin word meaning 'rain,' on the model of agriculture.

pneobiognosis [(puh-)nee-oh-bye-og-**noh**-siss] a rare medico-legal word for a test used to prove whether a child was born alive or dead, based on the presence or absence of air in the lungs. From Greek words meaning 'life' and 'knowledge.'

pococurantish [poh-koh-koo-**rahn**-tish] an adjective meaning careless or indifferent. From Latin words meaning 'little' and 'care.'

poculiform [**pah**-kyoo-li-form] an adjective meaning 'shaped like a cup.' The *-form* suffix, meaning 'having the shape of,' is remarkably productive, making it useful to people who can't bear to use a word like 'cup-shaped' when they could use a collateral adjective (one formed from a word collateral, or parallel, to the plain noun) instead. There's *drepaniform*, 'sickle-shaped,' *acetabuliform*, 'saucer-shaped,' *claviform*, 'club-shaped,' *hamiform*, 'hook-shaped,' *lacertiform*, 'lizard-shaped,' *moriform*, 'mulberry-shaped,' *patelliform*, 'kneecap-shaped,' *pugioniform*, 'dagger-shaped,' and *remiform*, 'oar-shaped.' Most of these words are used to describe the shapes of plant parts.

poffertje [**pah**-fur-tyuh] an Afrikaans word for a small doughnut dusted with sugar. The word ultimately comes from the French word *pouffer*, meaning 'to blow up.'

pogey [**poh**-ghee] an informal Canadian word meaning 'unemployment or welfare benefit,' as in "So you want me to end up on pogey?" It originally referred to a poorhouse or hostel for the needy or disabled: its current sense dates from the 1960s.

pokolpok [**pahk**-oll-**pahk**] a sacred Mayan ball game—the classical Mayan name was *pitz*. The object of the game was to put a rubber ball through a stone ring, using only hips, knees, and elbows.

poignet [**poyn**-yay] to put cuffs on a garment. From a French word meaning 'wrist' (although the cuffs themselves are not necessarily French ones).

173

pollinctor [pah-**lingk**-tur] a person who prepares a dead body for cremation or embalming. A nice, important-sounding synonym for *Funeral Director*. This comes from a Latin word meaning 'to wash a corpse.'

polissoir [**pol**-is-swar] a tool for buffing the fingernails. From a French word meaning 'a polishing instrument.'

polydipsia [pah-lee-**dip**-see-uh] abnormally great thirst. Also used figuratively, as in "a *polydipsia* for fame." From a Greek word meaning 'very thirsty.'

polynya [puh-lin-**yah**] an area of open water in the middle of an expanse of ice, especially in the Arctic. This word comes from a Russian word for the same thing, which comes from a root meaning 'field.' The plural is *polynyi*, if you come across more than one.

polyonym [**pah**-lee-uh-nim] the long-sought-after (almost-) synonym for *synonym*, it means 'each of a number of different words having the same meaning.' From a Greek word meaning 'having many names.'

pooking-fork [**pook**-ing-fork] a tool used in haymaking. It has a large prong and a cross handle, and it is used to push the hay into *pooks*, or stacks.

pooter [**poo**-tur] a suction bottle for collecting insects and other small invertebrates. A *pooter* has one tube through which insects are drawn into the bottle and another, protected by muslin or gauze, which is sucked. It is apparently named after F. W. Poos (1891–1987), an American entomologist.

possident [**pah**-si-duhnt] a rare term for a possessor, i.e., a person who owns something.

pregustator [pree-gus-**tay**-tur] a person whose job it is to taste meats and drinks before serving them. From a Latin word meaning 'to taste before.'

princock [**prin**-kok] a conceited young man. The *OED* says that the word was apparently slang, or "somewhat obscene" and that its origin is obscure.

pronk [prahngk] a weak or foolish person. This word is of uncertain origin, and it may come from a Dutch word meaning 'fop.' *Pronk* is also a verb used in South Africa of a springbok's leap in the air, especially as an alarm signal.

protologism [pro-**tol**-uh-jizm] a brand-new word, created in the hopes that others will pick it up and use it. A protologism is even newer than a neologism. Coined by Mikhail Epstein from the Greek words for 'first' and 'word.'

prunt [pruhnt] a small lump or piece of ornamental glass that is attached to another piece of glass (usually a bottle or vase). The glass is often dropped hot onto the surface being decorated, and then pressed with a tool (also called a *prunt*) like that used to make wax seals.

pruriginous [prur-**ridj**-ih-nus] irritable, uneasy, fretful. The *OED* has 'characterized by mental itching.' From a Latin word meaning 'to itch' and related to *prurigo*, a disease of the skin that causes terrible itching.

pseudogeusia [soo-duh-**gyoo**-shuh] the *OED* gives this as 'a false or perverted sense of taste.' A wonderful word when arguing with someone about what movie to see.

psilosopher [sye-**lah**-suh-fur] a person with a petty or shallow philosophy. From the Greek root *psilo-*, meaning 'bare, mere.'

psychopomp [**sye**-koh-pomp] someone or something that leads souls to the place of the dead. Also, a spiritual guide for a (living) person's soul; a person who acts as a guide of a soul. From Greek words meaning 'soul' and 'guide.' The adjective is *psychopompous*, but somehow that seems to demand a different definition.

POW!

DAD! He says it's IMPORTANT!

PSYCHOPOMP

pug-nozzle [**pug**-nozz-zle] to move the nostrils and upper lip in the manner of a pug dog.

puku [**poo**-koo] a colloquial New Zealand word meaning 'the stomach.' From a Maori word.

pulmentarious [pul-men-**tar**-ee-uhs] a rare word meaning 'made with gruel.'

pulsative [**pul**-suh-tiv] an adjective applied to musical instruments, meaning 'played by percussion.' It can also be used to mean 'being able to throb or pulse,' as a heart.

pulsiloge [**pul**-si-lohj] an obsolete device, usually a pendulum, used to measure someone's pulse. It was formed by analogy with *horologe*, an older word for 'timepiece' or 'clock.'

pulveratricious [pul-ver-uh-**tri**-shuhs] an adjective meaning 'like birds that roll themselves in dust,' usually used as a fancy way of saying 'dust-colored.'

pyknic [**pik**-nik] an adjective meaning 'stocky, with a rounded body and head, a thick trunk, and a tendency to fat.' It comes from a Greek word meaning 'thick,' and it was part of a system devised by Ernst Kretschmer (1888–1964) that correlated physical types with temperaments, criminal tendencies, and mental illness. The *pyknic* type was supposedly more prone to manic depression than the *leptosomic* (see **gammerstang**) type and tended towards crimes involving deception and fraud.

PULMENTARIOUS

quader [**kway**-der] an obsolete and rare word meaning 'to square a number.'

quadragenarian [kwah-druh-djuh-**nair**-ee-un] someone who is forty years old. One such person is described as "a stalwart well-oiled *quadragenarian*" in an *OED* citation from 1892. The adjective is *quadragenarious*, which is used in the 1895 citation "One of these plumply mellow *quadrigenarious* bodies."

quadragesimarian [kwah-druh-djess-uh-**mair**-ee-un] an obsolete and rare word meaning 'someone who observes Lent.' This certainly applies to those people who observe Lent only as an opportunity for a Friday fish fry as well as to those who take the more traditional and spiritual ascetic approach. The adjective *quaresimal* means 'having the qualities of Lenten fare; meager, austere.'

quadrumanous [kwah-**droom**-uh-nus] an adjective meaning 'ape-like in destructiveness.' From a Latin word meaning 'four-handed (like an ape).'

quaestuary [**kwess**-choo-err-ee] an adjective meaning 'money making.' Look for this word to show up in spam email any minute now.

quagswag [kwag-swag] an obsolete and rare word meaning 'to shake back and forth.'

quaintrelle [kwayn-**trel**] a well-dressed woman. A feminine form of a French word meaning 'beau, fop.'

qualtagh [**kwahl**-tuhkh] the first person you meet after leaving your house on some special occasion. Also, the first person entering a house on New Year's Day (often called a *first-foot*). The new year's *qualtagh*, for luck, is supposed to be a dark-haired man. A red-headed or female *qualtagh* is unlucky. Other things to bring luck to the house on New Year's Day include serving black-eyed peas, having the *qualtagh* bring shortbread and whiskey (sounds fine for any day of the year), and sweeping all the garbage in the house out through the front door before midnight on New Year's Eve (so that any of the misfortune of the past year is gone, not to return).

quangocrat [**kwang**-go-krat] a word found mostly in British English for a petty bureaucrat who works at a Quasi-Autonomous Non-Governmental Organization (or, acronymically, a *quango*).

quantophrenia [quahn-to-**free**-nee-uh] an obsessive reliance on mathematical methods or results, especially in social science research where they may not be strictly applicable.

quar [kwor] an obsolete word meaning 'to choke or fill up (a channel or passage).' Anyone who has a narrow hallway that seems to collect every random bicycle, awkward pair of shoes, and child's toy possible has a use for this word.

quatervois [kwah-ter-**vwah**] an obsolete and rare word meaning 'a crossroads, a place where four ways meet.' Influenced by French words meaning 'four' and 'way.'

R

raccolta [ruh-**kohl**-tuh] an obsolete word meaning 'a collection, a crop or harvest.' From an Italian word meaning 'to collect.'

rachisagra [rack-uh-**sag**-ruh] pain in the spine. From a Greek word meaning 'spine.'

rackensak [**rack**-in-sack] a possibly obsolete word meaning 'a native of Arkansas.'

rassasy [ruh-**say**-zee] to satisfy a hungry person. This word is related to *satiate*, and they come from the same Latin root meaning 'enough.'

rastaquouère [rahs-tuh-**kwerr**] a social climber who tries too hard to be in fashion, especially one from a South American or Mediterranean country. Also, an exciting but untrustworthy stranger. From an American Spanish word meaning 'upstart.'

rataplan [rat-uh-**plan**] a drumming noise. A verb, it means 'to beat a drum.' From an onomatopoeic French word of the same meaning.

ratomorphic [rat-oh-**mor**-fick] a rare word meaning 'someone who refuses to believe that people have any mental processes that can't be shown to exist in lower animals.' From *rat*, on the model of *anthropomorphic*.

RASSASY

ravigote [rah-vee-**gawt**] the herbs tarragon, chervil, chives, and bur-net, which, when used together, were supposed to have the power of resuscitation. From a French word meaning 'to invigorate.'

rawky [**raw**-kee] a rare adjective which means 'foggy, damp, and cold,' as in a *rawky day* or *rawky weather*. It comes from *roke*, a dialect word for mist, fog, or drizzly rain.

relexification [ree-**leck**-si-fi-**kay**-shun] a term from linguistics which means 'the process of replacing a word or phrase in one language with the corresponding word or phrase from another language, without changing the grammar of the items introduced.' *I am très impressed* is an example of relexification of the French word *très* into English.

rememble [ri-**mem**-ble] a false memory, especially of some place, object, or event of one's childhood. Also used as a verb: "I *remembled* the house as being bigger, and not so yellow." Possibly a blend of *fumble* and *remember*. This word was coined by Elan Cole, who suggested it on the radio show *The Next Big Thing*.

retardataire [ri-tar-duh-**terr**] an adjective meaning behind the times, or characteristic of an earlier period. Used mainly about artistic styles, it seems useful to describe people with fossilized hairdos: "She's so *retardataire*—when was the last time you saw a beehive like that?" The word comes from a French word meaning 'one who is late in arriving.'

retcon [**ret**-kahn] an often-condemned practice of writers for televi-sion and other serial stories, such as comic books, in which they men-tion previously unknown events in order to justify current plot points. The word is a blend of the words *retroactive* and *continuity*.

retrochoir [**ret**-ro-kwyer] not, as one might imagine, a group that only sings old church music, but instead the part of a cathedral or other large church that is behind the high altar.

retroition [ret-roh-**i**-shuhn] a rare word that means 'the action of returning; re-entrance.' Finally, a word for that embarrassing return to a party, after all goodbyes have been said, to retrieve an essential item left behind (usually one's keys, making the retroition completely unavoidable).

rettery [**ret**-er-ee] a place where flax is retted, or soaked and softened. Retting flax produces a very pungent, unpleasant odor, and *ret* and *rettery* are related to the word *rot*.

retund [ri-**tund**] to blunt the sharp edge of a weapon, or to weaken something. A rare and obsolete word, it comes from a Latin word meaning 'to strike again.'

revolera [re-vo-**le**-ruh] a word for the fluttering of the cape above the matador's head. The more stereotypical bullfighting move of flapping the cape behind one's back is called *mariposa*, Spanish for 'butterfly.'

rhagades [**rag**-uh-deez] a plural noun meaning 'cracked or sore patches on the skin.' It comes from a Greek word meaning 'rent' (as in tear) or 'chink.'

rhathymia [ruh-**thye**-mee-uh] the state of being cheerful, merry, and optimistic. It comes from a Greek word meaning 'to take a vacation, be idle.'

RHYPAROGRAPHER

rhedarious [ri-**derr**-ee-uhs] a rare adjective meaning 'used as a cart or chariot.' If you pile things on your wheeled office chair to move them down the hall, your chair is then *rhedarious*. It comes from a Latin word for a kind of four-wheeled carriage.

rhinarium [rye-**nerr**-ee-uhm] the hairless and moist nose of some mammals.

rhineurynter [**rine**-yoo-rin-ter] an inflatable bag used to plug the nose. This seems to have some medical application, and is not, as one might think, a murder weapon or an instrument of torture. It comes from Greek words meaning 'nose' and 'to broaden.'

rhyparographer [rip-uh-**rah**-gruh-fer] a painter of unpleasant or sordid subjects. From Greek words meaning 'filthy' and 'writer.'

rhytidectomy [rye-ti-**deck**-tuh-mee] the surgical removal of wrinkles, especially from the face. Used also as a technical term for 'face-lift.' From Greek words meaning 'wrinkle' and 'cutting.'

ribaldail [**rib**-ul-dale] an obsolete word meaning 'common fellows, low company.' From the same (obscure) root as *ribald*. In the royal household of France there used to be an officer called the *king of the ribalds,* who had jurisdiction over all the brothels and gaming-houses around the court.

ribazuba [ree-buh-**zoo**-buh] an obsolete word for walrus ivory. From Russian words meaning 'fish' and 'tooth.'

rimbombo [rim-**bahm**-boh] a rare word meaning 'a booming roar.' To *rimbomb* is 'to echo or resound.'

Ringerike [**ring**-uh-reek-uh] a style of late Viking art that used lots of plant motifs. Which, if you ever thought of Viking art in the first place, would have certainly seemed unlikely. The word comes from a place in Norway north of Oslo.

rixation [rick-**say**-shun] an obsolete word meaning 'scolding, fighting.' From a Latin word meaning 'to quarrel.'

rockoon [rah-**koon**] a rocket fired from a balloon, or a balloon carrying a rocket. A blend of *rocket* and *balloon*.

roinish [**roy**-nish] an obsolete word meaning 'scabby, coarse, despicable.' *Roin* is an obsolete word meaning 'scab.'

rosicler [**rose**-i-clear] the rosy light of dawn.

roucoulement [roo-cool-**mahn**] a rare word meaning 'the gentle cooing of doves,' of course also extended to mean the soft voices of women. From a French word of the same meaning.

Sabaism [**say**-bay-iz-um] the worship and adoration of the stars. From a Hebrew word meaning 'host.'

sachentege [**satch**-un-tej] a torture device describe in the Anglo-Saxon Chronicle as "fastened to a beam, having a sharp iron to go round the throat and neck, so that the person tortured could in no wise sit, lie, or sleep, but that he must at all times bear all the iron."

salebrosity [sal-uh-**brah**-si-tee] 'unevenness, roughness.' From a Latin word of the same meaning.

samentale [**sah**-mun-tale] a obsolete word meaning 'agreement.' It seems to come from the phrase 'of the same tale.'

sandapile [san-**duh**-puh-lee] an obsolete word meaning 'a coffin.'

sanguinolency [sang-**gwin**-uh-lun-see] an obsolete word meaning 'addiction to bloodshed.' Thankfully, most of the *sanguinolent* these days can satisfy their jones for gore with videogames and movies. From a Latin word meaning 'blood.'

sarcinarious [sahr-si-**nair**-ee-us] an obsolete word meaning 'able to to carry burdens or loads.' From a Latin word meaning 'bundle.'

Sardanapalian [sahrd-nuh-**pay**-lee-un] an adjective meaning 'luxuriously effeminate.' From the name of Sardanapalus, the last king of Nineveh, who was supposed to have lived in outrageous luxury. Beseiged by the Medes for two years, his favorite concubine induced him to put himself on a funeral pyre. She set fire to it herself and it consumed the palace and his entire court. The legend of Sardanapalus cannot be connected with any Assyrian king known through archaeology.

Sardoodledom [sahr-**doo**-dle-dum] a word used to describe well-written and clever, but trivial or immoral, plays, or the milieu in which such work is praised. From the name of French playwright Victorien Sardou (1831–1908). His best-known farce is *Divorçons (Let's Get a Divorce)* (1880), in which a married woman, hearing about a new divorce law about to be passed, starts a flirtation with her husband's cousin. The cousin deceives her with a telegram, implying that the law has been passed. The woman then suggests a friendly divorce to her husband, who agrees and resumes his bachelor life, which makes the woman jealous. The woman and her husband dine in private together and reconcile, leaving the cousin alone and discomfited.

sarvodaya [sahr-**voh**-duh-yuh] a word meaning 'the well-being of all.' Used by Gandhi (1869–1948) to mean a new social order without caste, based on nonviolence and service. From a Sanskrit word meaning 'prosperity.'

satisdiction [sat-is-**dick**-shun] a word meaning 'saying enough.' If only we knew to shut up after achieving *satisdiction*. From Latin words meaning 'enough' and 'saying,' on the model of *satisfaction*. Another 'enough' word is *satispassion*, which means 'atonement by adequate suffering,' which leads to the burning question: "How much suffering is enough?" Especially the suffering caused by someone who never seems to reach *satisdiction*.

Satanophany [say-tuh-**nah**-fuh-nee] a visible manifestation of Satan. From *Satan*, obviously, and the same *-phany* as in *epiphany*, from a Greek word meaning 'manifestation.'

savernapron [say-ver-**nay**-pruhn] a table-napkin. A corruption of an old French word meaning 'save-tablecloth.'

scabilonian [skab-uh-**loh**-nee-un] the *OED* glosses this word as 'a contemptuous term for some kind of garment.'

scacchic [**skack**-ick] a rare adjective meaning 'of or pertaining to chess.' From an Italian word meaning 'chess.'

scamander [skuh-**man**-der] to wander about. A rare word, it apparently comes from *Skamandros*, the name of a river in Homer's *Iliad*. Another, more familiar English word with the same meaning is *meander*: this is also based on the name of a different river, the *Menderes*, known in ancient times as the *Maiandros*.

scelestious [si-**less**-chus] a rare adjective meaning 'wicked.' Another form is *scelestic*. They both come from a Latin word with the same meaning.

scevity [**see**-vuh-tee] an obsolete word meaning 'unluckiness.' It comes (like so many "unlucky" words do) from a Latin word with a 'left' meaning—in this case 'left-sided, awkward.'

schismogenesis [sizz-moh-**jen**-uh-sis] the differentiation between people, social groups, or cultures caused by reciprocal exaggerated responses to each other's behavior. Everyone is familiar with the classic relationship example: one person has a fear of abandonment, the other a fear of commitment, and every advance in intimacy is met by a pulling back, leading to more pursuit and many, many bad romantic comedies. Falling in love can be considered a kind of inverted *schismogenesis;* instead of differentiation, assimilation. From a Greek word meaning 'rift, cleft' and -*genesis*.

Schrecklichkeit [**shreck**-likh-kite] a deliberate policy of terrorizing non-combatants. Sometimes used figuratively, as in this citation from 1977: "The Schrecklichkeit in which the relations between parents and children are so often conducted in Britain."

sciapodous [sye-**app**-uh-dus] having feet large enough to shelter the whole body when used as an umbrella. From a Greek word meaning 'shadow foot.' The *Sciapodes* who had these feet were supposed to live in Libya.

sciatherical [sye-uh-**theer**-i-kul] an adjective meaning 'concerned with the recording of shadows, especially the shadow of the sun as a means for telling time.' From a Greek word for sundial, literally 'shadow-catcher.'

scibility [si-**bil**-uh-tee] an obsolete word meaning 'the power of knowing.' From a Latin word meaning 'able to know.'

scleragogy [**skleer**-uh-gah-jee] severe training or punishment of the body. From Greek roots meaning 'hard' and 'guiding.'

scofflaw [**skahf**-law] someone who contemptuously breaks the law, especially a law that's difficult to enforce. This isn't a very rare word, but it has a marvelous origin. A Massachusetts man, Delcevare King of Quincy, held a contest in 1923 to find a word for the 'lawless drinker' of illegal alcohol, and he offered $200 as a prize. He received 25,000 entries, coming from all over the United States and from several foreign countries. Two entrants, Mr. Henry Irving Dale and Miss Kate L. Butler, independently came up with *scofflaw*, and they split the prize on January 15, 1924.

scolecophagous [skah-li-**koff**-uh-gus] worm eating. Used mostly about birds (especially early ones) but ripe for extended, metaphorical, or figurative use.

scollardicall [skuh-**lahr**-di-kle] an adjective supposed to be an illiterate epithet for a learned person.

scopperil [**skop**-uh-ril] a hyperactive child, or a squirrel. From another use of the word to mean 'a kind of spinning top.'

scopperloit [**skah**-per-loit] a time for play, or rude or rough-housing play. Of obscure origin.

scoteography [skoh-tee-**ogg**-ruh-fee] the art of writing in the dark. From Greek words meaning 'darkness' and 'writing.'

scowbanker [**skow**-bank-er] a dishonest or unscrupulous merchant.

scramasax [**skram**-uh-saks] a large hunting and battle knife used by the Franks.

scriniary [**skrye**-nee-err-ee] a keeper of the archives, an archivist. From a Latin word meaning 'a box for books and papers; a writing desk.'

scrimshandrix [**skrim**-shan-driks] a rare word meaning a woman who makes scrimshaw (carvings on ivory or bone, often done by sailors). The masculine term is *scrimshander*, another term in use (or as much use as it can hope to get) is *scrimshoner*, and the process of making scrimshaw can be called *scrimshonting*. The origin of the word isn't known, but it may have come from the name *Scrimshaw*.

scripophily [skrip-**ah**-fi-lee] the collecting of stock and bond certificates, not as investments, but as works of art or because of the issuing company's historical or economic significance. The word comes from *scrip*, 'stock certificate,' and *-phily*.

scrippage [**skrip**-ij] one's baggage and personal belongings. William Shakespeare invented the word, using it in the phrase 'scrip and scrippage,' on the pattern of 'bag and baggage'; a *scrip* was a small bag or pouch carried by a pilgrim, shepherd, or beggar.

scriptitation [skrip-ti-**tay**-shun] an obsolete and rare word meaning 'continuous writing.' From a Latin word meaning 'to write.' *Scriptitation* is what you wish your favorite authors would do.

selcouth [**sel**-kooth] an adjective meaning 'unfamiliar, rare, strange, marvelous, wonderful.' It comes from Old English words meaning 'seldom known.' *Uncouth* and *selcouth* used to be synonyms, but uncouth now means 'unpleasant, rude.' Another rare, etymologically overdetermined word meaning 'rare' is *rarachose*, which comes from French *rare chose*, 'rare thing.'

semihiant [sem-ee-**hye**-unt] an adjective meaning '(of lips) half-open.' Much, much nicer than *agape* or *slack-jawed*. The one citation for this word in the *OED* shows that it's very nice: "He stooped and kissed the *semihiant* lips."

semiopathy [se-mee-**ah**-puh-thee] the tendency to read humorously inappropriate meanings into signs. One anecdote is about the literary critic Terry Eagleton (1943–). He saw a sign next to an escalator reading "Dogs Must Be Carried." Since he wanted to go upstairs, he went off to find a dog. Other fine examples are "Slow Children Crossing" and "The Door Is Alarmed." The word seems to have been coined by the editors of the "Feedback" section of *New Scientist* magazine.

semordnilap [sem-**ord**-nih-lap] a word that spells a different word when written backwards (*semordnilap* is *palindromes* spelled backwards). *Drawer* is a semordnilap, because backwards it spells *reward*. If this makes you uneasy, you might have *aibohphobia*, 'fear of palindromes.'

sengilbond [**seng**-gul-bond] an obsolete and rare word meaning 'an encircling band.' Someone should snap this up as a trade name for those plastic straps that hold shipping cartons shut—the ones that are nearly impossible to remove unless you attempt to use them as carrying handles, in which case they disobligingly snap open immediately.

seplasiary [si-**play**-zee-err-ee] a perfumer. This word comes from the name of a street in Capua in Southern Italy where perfume was sold.

sericipary [se-ri-**sip**-er-ee] an adjective meaning 'producing silk,' from Latin roots meaning 'silk' and 'birth.'

sericon [**serr**-i-kahn] a substance supposed to be involved in the process of changing base metals into gold. Obviously, there is no basis for connecting this substance with zinc, which was done by some writers of the eighteenth century.

sermocination [ser-moh-si-**nay**-shuhn] an extremely irritating rhetorical device in which the speaker, having asked a question, immediately answers it. The words *sermocinator* and *sermocinatrix* mean 'speaker' and 'female speaker,' respectively.

shamal [shuh-**mahl**] a hot, dry, north-westerly wind blowing across the Persian Gulf in summer and typically causing sandstorms. The term comes from the Arabic word for 'north.' The *simoom* is another hot, dry wind that blows in this part of the world: it takes its name from an Arabic word meaning 'to poison.'

shammade [shuh-**mayd**] a rare and obsolete Scottish word meaning 'to ornament with lace.'

shandrydan [**shan**-dree-dan] a humorous term for any kind of rickety or old-fashioned vehicle. Of obscure origin, but probably related to *shandry cart*, a light cart on springs.

siagonology [sye-uh-guh-**nah**-luh-jee] the study of jawbones, especially in order to deduce personality traits or racial characteristics. From a Greek root meaning 'jaw.'

sincanter [sin-**kan**-ter] an obsolete and derogatory term of abuse, applied to men. It is usually in the phrase "old sincanter." Its origin is obscure.

STRANGE AND
SENSATIONAL SERVANTS

If words are the servants of thoughts, words for servants should serve some weird and wonderful thinking, if only of the "why?", "how?", and "huh?" variety.

Harlots are attended by their *apple-squires,* and greyhounds by their *fewterers;* ship's surgeons have their *loblolly boys,* and Roman magistrates their *apparitors.* Indian landowners have a *chuprassy* or two hanging around, wearing their official badges in splendor, and every bluestocking employs a *lectrice* to read aloud. Scholars and magicians have at least one *famulus,* to keep the place suitably untidy and obtain impossible things at short notice. A bullfighter has a *mozo,* and a priest has a *crucifer* to do the heavy lifting of carrying a cross in procession.

Someone who attends a bedchamber is a *cubicular;* someone who attends a bath is a *topass.* Someone who cuts your bread at the table is a *trenchpaine.* The *scrape-trencher* did just that. In India, the head of your pantry and kitchen is a *khansamah,* and a general table servant is a *khidmutgar.* The *squiller* is in charge of the scullery. A *mediastine* is a kitchen drudge. The *manciple* purchases provisions for a college or a monastery.

Military attendants, or those dressed in military or huntsman style, like *chasseurs* and *jaegers,* are always popular. *Escuderos* bear shields, or are ladies' pages; a *coistrel* is in charge of the horses of a knight (and is also a 'low varlet'). If you want your servant to run secret errands, wearing gray instead of your normal livery, you have a *grison* in your employ. An armed courier (especially in Turkey) is a *kavass*. A *pandour* is much the same, only in Croatia and Hungary. A *wanlasour* drives the game back toward you for ease of shooting. A *ferash* will spread your carpet and pitch your tent, among other things. A *piqueur* will run before your carriage to clear the road. A *syce* will tend to your horses and follow your carriage on foot. A *mussalchee* will carry a torch for you (but only in the literal sense).

> **Scholars and magicians have at least one *famulus*, to keep the place suitably untidy and obtain impossible things at short notice.**

If you just need a general servant, you can hire an *attendress,* an *underlout,* a *backman* or *jackman,* a *knape,* a *tindal,* a *pedissequent,* a *valect,* or (if you want one for unscrupulous duties only) a *myrmidon.* Where do you find your servants, especially your *schelchenes,* or servant girls? Well, you can try your local *giglet-fair.* Don't forget to pay them their *arles,* or hiring bonus, to confirm their engagement. They will expect to have their *kist,* or trunk, sent for as well.

sindonology [sin-duh-**nah**-luh-jee] the study of the Shroud of Turin.

singerie [san-zhuh-**ree**] a decorative style using pictures of monkeys, often wearing clothes or indulging in other anthropomorphic behavior. From a French word meaning 'monkey business; a collection of monkeys.'

singultus [sing-**gul**-tus] a rare word meaning 'a sob.' From a Latin word meaning 'speech broken by sobs.' *Singultient* is a rare word that means 'sobbing.'

sitooterie [sit-**oot**-uh-ree] a summerhouse or gazebo; also an out-of-the-way corner to sit with your partner during a dance. The word means 'a place to sit out' and comes from *sit* plus *oot* (Scots pronunciation of 'out') and the noun ending -*erie*.

skeuomorph [**skyoo**-oh-morf] a decoration that takes its form from the nature of the material used or the method used to make it. The word is also used for an object that copies the design of a similar object made in another material— a plastic Adirondack chair would be a *skeuomorph*. From Greek words meaning 'form' and 'vessel.'

slangrel [**slang**-grul] an obsolete and rare word meaning 'a lean or long person or thing.'

sleck [slek] soft mud, ooze. *Sleck* is supposedly finer and smoother than sludge to the discerning mind (or foot).

small-back [**smawl**-bak] an allusion to Death, because he is often drawn as a skeleton. Another, similar name for Death was *dustyfoot*.

snite [snyt] a dialect and Scottish word meaning to wipe or blow the nose. It may also mean 'to put out a candle.' It is probably related to *snout* and *snot*.

snollygoster [**snah**-lee-gahs-ter] a dishonest politician, especially a shrewd or calculating one. A connection has been proposed between this word and *snallygaster*, a mythical monster of Maryland, invented to frighten freed slaves. However, the first evidence for *snallygaster* follows *snollygoster* by about a hundred years, making a connection (in this direction, at least) unlikely.

solfeggist [sol-**fedj**-ist] someone who sings notes using do (or ut), re, mi, fa, sol, la, and si (or ti). From the names of the notes *sol* and *fa*.

solander [suh-**lan**-der] a protective box, made in the form of a book, for holding items such as botanical specimens, maps, and color plates. The word comes from the name of Daniel C. Solander, an eighteenth-century Swedish botanist.

solein [**sah**-layn] an adjective meaning 'done alone, in privacy or solitude.' A lonesome-sounding word, it comes from the same root as *sole*, and the word *sullen* is descended from it. It seems that if you do too much alone, you become sullen.

soucouyant [soo-koo-**yahn**] in the Eastern Caribbean, witch who sheds her skin at night and sucks the blood of her victims.

souspirable [soo-spi-**rah**-bluh] lamentable, deplorable. From a French word meaning 'to sigh.'

souteneur [sut-uh-**ner**] an old word for 'pimp,' or a man who lives on the earnings of prostitutes. From a French word meaning 'protector.'

SPANGHEW

spanghew [**spang**-hyoo] to cause a frog or toad to fly into the air. (Usually violently, from the end of a stick, although it seems as though it wouldn't ever feel gentle to the poor toad or frog!) Of obscure origin.

spartle [**spahr**-tul] a Scottish word meaning 'to move the body in a sprawling or struggling way, to thrash around.'

sparto-statics [**spahr**-toh-**stat**-icks] the study of the strength of ropes. Since there is only one citation in the *OED* for this word, it's amusing to imagine the melodramatic death of the would-be sparto-statician, who, having misjudged a particular rope's strength, goes plummeting over the cliff.

spawling [**spawl**-ing] an archaic word for the act of spitting, or the results of spitting. The word *spawl* means 'to spit copiously.'

spouch [spowch] unwanted messages sent through a haptic system. A haptic system delivers physical sensations, especially touch and texture, by artificial means. Videogame controllers that jolt you when your avatar suffers a violent death and cellphones that vibrate in particular patterns are both haptic systems. The idea is that, as these systems get more sophisticated, they will be hijacked by people with less benign intentions. Imagine thinking you're about to hold hands with your sweetie through a haptic system in your phone and instead feeling the steering wheel of a car in some advertisement. *Spouch* is a blend of *spam* and *touch* and right now is completely theoretical.

spumescence [spyoo-**mes**-uhns] foaminess, frothiness.

squassation [skwah-**say**-shuhn] a severe shaking. From an Italian word with the same meaning.

SQUINTIFEGO

squintifego [skwin-ti-**fee**-goh] a person who squints very much.

squirk [skwerk] a half-suppressed laugh. Of imitative origin.

stafador [**staff**-uh-dore] a obsolete and rare word meaning 'an impostor.' From a Spanish word meaning 'to swindle.'

starchitect [**stahr**-ki-tekt] a star architect. Usually used derisively, as in "The defining characteristic of the *starchitects* is their utter disregard for the laws of physics and the people who will actually use the building."

steganography [steg-uh-**nahg**-ruh-fee] the art of secret writing; cryptography. This word is now usually used to mean the practice of hiding secret data by encoding it electronically in another, innocuous file. Sometimes it's abbreviated as *stego*. How is it related to the other *stego*, the *stegosaurus*? They both come from a Greek word meaning 'covered.' In *steganography*, the writing is covered up; the *stegosaurus* is covered in bony plates.

stelk [stelk] a dish made of onions and mashed potatoes, with a large lump (often an entire pound) of butter or lard in the middle of it. It's an Irish dish and is also called *champ*.

stellionate [**stel**-yuh-nuht] a legal term for fraud committed in making contracts, especially that which involves selling the same thing (or rights to the same thing) to different persons, often a thing that is not the fraudster's possession to begin with. So, not just selling the Brooklyn Bridge, but selling it twice. This comes from a Latin word meaning 'a fraudulent person' and may be derived from a word for a kind of lizard.

stenotopic [sten-uh-**top**-ik] an adjective meaning 'able to tolerate only a restricted range of ecological conditions or habitats.' So your relative who must have the window open exactly five inches and who cannot eat anything but plain chicken breast and steamed broccoli? *Stenotopic.*

steracle [**sterr**-uh-kul] an obsolete word meaning 'a spectacle or show.' This word may come from the word *stare*, modeled on *spectacle*.

sternutation [ster-n(y)oo-**tay**-shuhn] the act of sneezing or a sneeze. From a Latin word with the same meaning, this word is used mostly in medical contexts, or by people trying to be funny. Something that causes sneezing is *sternutatory*; a medicine that causes sneezing is *errhine*.

stilo novo [**stee**-lo **noh**-vo] when used with a date, this means 'according to the Gregorian calendar.' It's also used figuratively to mean any innovation. From Latin words meaning 'new style.'

stoop-gallant [**stoop**-gal-uhnt] a disease or illness. A historical term, it originally referred specifically to the sweating sicknesses prevalent in England in the fifteenth and sixteenth centuries and is presumably meant to suggest that such illnesses would bring 'gallants,' i.e., fine gentlemen, to their knees with weakness and exhaustion.

storiation [stor-ee-**ay**-shun] decoration of something with designs that represent historical, legendary, or symbolic subjects. Practically every public mural has some kind of *storiation*.

STOOP-GALLANT

stylite [**stye**-lite] a Christian ascetic who lived standing on top of a pillar in ancient times, permanently exposed to the elements, and dependent on others for food and drink brought up by ladder. The word comes from *stulos*, the Greek for 'pillar,' and the first and best-known *stylite*, or pillar saint, was St. Simeon Stylites, who spent thirty years living in this way.

subumber [sub-**um**-ber] an obsolete and rare word meaning 'to shelter.' However, the word *subumbrage* means 'to overshadow.' Both words are related to *umbrella*, and come from a Latin word meaning 'shade.'

sudorific [soo-duh-**riff**-ik] an adjective meaning 'causing perspiration,' either through effort or in a medical way. Also, thankfully more rarely, 'consisting of sweat.'

sukebind [**s(y)ook**-bind] an imaginary plant used by Stella Gibbons in *Cold Comfort Farm*, associated with superstition and fertility, especially (as the *OED* puts it) 'intense rustic passions.'

superbious [soo-**per**-bee-uhs] a very rare adjective meaning 'proud and overbearing.' It comes from a Latin word meaning 'proud or magnificent,' as does the familiar English adjective *superb*.

supputation [sup-yoo-**tay**-shuhn] the act of computing or calculating. From a Latin word meaning 'count up.'

surbater [sur-**bay**-ter] an obsolete and rare word for 'someone who tires another person with walking.' According to most young children, all parents are *surbaters*.

surfle [**sur**-fle] a face wash or cosmetic. Obviously predating the development of product naming or brand awareness. *Surfle* can also mean 'to embroider,' and comes from a Latin word that means 'thread on top.'

sursaut [sur-**sawt**] in the phrase *a sursaut* this means 'all of a sudden.' Also, as a verb, 'to attack suddenly.' From a Latin word meaning 'leap.'

swabble [**swah**-ble] to make a noise like water being sloshed around.

swanimote [**swah**-nuh-mote] a special court, formerly held fifteen days before Michaelmas. It was originally one where forest officers superintended the departure of pigs and cattle and sheep from the king's woods so that they didn't interfere with the hunting. From a Latin word meaning 'a meeting of swineherds.'

swan-upping [**swahn**-up-ing] the task of marking swans by nicking their beaks, to brand them as being owned by the crown or a company.

swartrutter [**swort**-rut-er] a mercenary soldier who wore black clothes and armor and blackened his face. The *OED* notes that they "infested the Netherlands in the 16th and 17th centuries." Literally, 'black trooper.'

swasivious [sway-**siv**-ee-us] an obsolete or rare word meaning 'agreeably persuasive.' Much better than being disagreeably persuasive, in the action-movie, gun-to-the-head way.

swayamvara [sway-uhm-**vah**-ruh] a Hindu ceremony in which a woman chooses her husband from several candidates, or a symbolic version of this before an arranged marriage. The girl signals her choice by giving him a garland of flowers. From Sanskrit words meaning 'self choice.'

swazzle [**swah**-zle] a mouthpiece used by a puppeteer to make the squeaking voice of Mr. Punch.

sweeny [**swee**-nee] a word meaning 'atrophy of the shoulder (in a horse)' but used figuratively to mean 'stiff with pride or self-importance.' From a German word meaning 'atrophy.'

sychnocarpous [sik-no-**kahr**-puhs] an adjective meaning 'bearing fruit many times.'

sycomancy [**sik**-uh-man-see] divination by means of figs or fig-leaves.

213

taniwha [**tan**-i-wah] a mythical monster that, according to Maori legend, lives in very deep water.

tappen [**tap**-uhn] the plug by which the rectum of a bear is closed during hibernation: according to J. G. Wood in an 1865 volume of *Illustrated Natural History*, 'the tappen is almost entirely composed of pine-leaves, and the various substances which the Bear scratches out of the ants' nests.' There is no contemporary evidence of the word's use and no further information to be found regarding the composition of the plug!

tegestology [tej-es-**tah**-luh-jee] the collecting of beer mats. Irregularly formed from a Latin word meaning 'covering, mat.'

telautograph [tel-**aw**-tuh-graf] a forgotten offshoot of the telegraph in which writing done with a pen or pencil at the transmitter is reproduced at the receiving end by communicating movements to the receiving pen. There are no citations in the *OED* after 1905. From a Greek root meaning 'distance' and autograph.

tellurian [tuh-**loor**-ee-uhn] an adjective meaning 'of or inhabiting the earth.' The word is also used as a noun to mean 'an inhabitant of the earth,' especially in science fiction: it comes from a Latin word meaning 'the earth.'

telmatology [tel-muh-**tah**-luh-jee] the study of peat-bogs. The adjective for peat-boggian, if needed, is *turbarian*, and the Scottish dialect word for peat-bog is *yarpha*.

telpherage [**tel**-fer-ij] a system where minerals or other goods are transported in buckets suspended from a cable and moved by an electric motor supplied with current from an adjacent conductor. From Greek roots meaning 'distance' and 'bearing.'

temulent [**tem**-yoo-luhnt] an adjective meaning 'drunken' or 'intoxicating,' from Latin roots meaning 'intoxicating drink' and 'wine.'

tendsome [**tend**-suhm] a possibly imaginary word, supposedly meaning 'requiring much attendance.' This is a word that, for a while, was only known through dictionary entries; two from *Webster* (in 1847 and 1864) and one from the *Century Dictionary* (1891). Not that lexicographers ever put in words maliciously, but occasionally a word that looks all right will slip through, like an uninvited guest. And, with words as with people, once they're seen in the right crowd, other parties (and other dictionaries) become open to them. And once they're in dictionaries writers often pick them up. In fact, Steve Dodson, when copyediting this book, was curious enough to go search for a citation for it, and found not one but two, from 1860 and 1916.

testudineous [tes-t(y)oo-**din**-ee-us] an adjective meaning 'as slow as a tortoise.' From a Latin word meaning 'tortoise.'

tetrabard [**tet**-ruh-bard] a unit of measurement devised by Steven Pinker, in his book *The Language Instinct*. One bard equals 15,000 words, the number used in the complete works of Shakespeare; a *tetrabard* is 60,000 words, which Pinker considered to be the average vocabulary of a high-school graduate in the U.S. *New Scientist* magazine also printed a different unit of the bard scale, the *centibard*, submitted by teacher David Ridpath.

textome [**teks**-tohm] a word used to describe a body of literature, usually scientific research and articles, that can be analyzed by software developed to find meaning and information in texts. From 'text' plus the suffix *–ome,* which was a backformation from *genomics.*

textonym [**teks**-tuh-nim] the set of words that can be made from a particular sequence of keys pressed on a phone, where each number corresponds to several letters, especially when the phone uses predictive software to guess what you want. For instance, the sequence 5-4-7-7 provides both *lips* and *kiss*—a challenge for the software!

thalassic [thuh-**las**-ik] an adjective meaning 'relating to the sea,' from the Greek for sea, *thalassa*. Many of today's health and beauty centers offer *thalassotherapy*, which is the use of seawater for various therapeutic and cosmetic purposes.

thelytokous [thuh-**lit**-uh-kuhs] an adjective meaning 'producing only female offspring.' It is usually used to refer to the offspring of parthenogenesis, but there's no reason why its meaning can't be extended to the offspring of more conventional conception. From Greek roots meaning 'bearing' and 'female.' The word for having only male offspring is *arrenotokous*.

theoplasm [**thee**-oh-plaz-um] a rare word meaning 'the stuff of which gods are made.'

theopneust [**thee**-uhp-n(y)oost] an adjective meaning 'divinely inspired.' From Greek roots meaning 'God' and 'breathe.'

therblig [**ther**-blig] in time and motion study, any task that can be analyzed. This is an anagram of the name Gilbreth, from F. B. Gilbreth, an American engineer who was very influential in the field of motion study. (His children wrote two books about growing up in the home of a motion-study expert: *Cheaper by the Dozen* and *Belles on Their Toes*.)

therianthropy [**theer**-ee-**an**-throh-pee] a feeling of psychological or spiritual identification with a particular animal. People who feel this way call themselves *therianthropes* or *therians*, and may consider themselves to have animal or part-animal souls. The species of animal with which a particular therian identifies is sometimes referred to as their *theriotype*. From Greek words meaning 'wild animal' and 'man.'

thixotropy [thik-**sah**-truh-pee] the property of certain gels of becoming liquid when agitated and turning into a gel again when allowed to stand. From a German word with the same meaning, from Greek roots meaning 'touching' and 'turning.'

thurse [thurs] an obsolete word used to refer to giants in heathen mythology, or goblins and hobgoblins.

thwarterous [**thwort**-er-uhs] an adjective meaning 'twisted, gnarled.' A nonce-word irregularly formed from *thwart* on the model of *boisterous*.

tigon [**tye**-guhn] the hybrid offspring of a male tiger and a lion. A *liger* is the offspring produced by a male lion and a tigress.

timenoguy [**tim**-ih-nog-ee] a nautical word for a thingamig or gadget. Also spelled *Timmy-noggy*. From a French word for 'rudder' and *guy*, meaning 'rope.'

titivil [**tit**-uh-vul] a name for a devil said to collect words mumbled, dropped, or omitted in the recitation of divine service, and to carry them to hell where they would be held against the offender. By extension, a tattletale.

tmesis [**t(uh)mee**-sis] the separation of the parts of a compound word by the interposition of another word or words. From a Greek root meaning 'cutting.' The *OED* gives the example, 'How bright the chit and chat!'

tokoloshe [toh-kuh-**loh**-shee] in African folklore, a mischievous and lascivious hairy water sprite. The word comes from the Sesotho, Xhosa, and Zulu languages.

Torschlusspanik [**tor**-shloos-pan-ik] a German word (one of those concepts, like *Schadenfreude* or *Sprachgefühl*, that English, too lazy to come up with an Anglo-Saxon word, appropriates the German for) meaning 'a sense of panic in middle age brought on by the feeling that life is passing you by.' It literally means 'shut door panic.'

TORSCHLUSSPANIK

OUT

IN

tracasserie [truh-**kas**-uh-ree] a state of annoyance or a petty quarrel. This comes from a French word meaning 'to worry oneself.' A citation in the *OED* from 1879 reads "Life seems to me empty of all but *tracasseries*."

tractatrix [trak-**tay**-triks] a female shampooer. It is not recommended that you ask for the services of such a person by this term at your beauty parlor, salon, or barbershop, to avoid embarrassing misunderstandings.

tragelaph [**trag**-uh-laf] a fictional beast that was part goat and part stag. From Greek roots meaning 'he-goat' and 'stag.'

tragematopolist [truh-ghe-muh-**tah**-puh-list] a deservedly rare word meaning 'a seller of candy.' From a Greek word meaning 'dried fruit or candy.'

tralatitious [tral-uh-**tish**-uhs] an adjective meaning 'traditional, handed down from generation to generation.' From a Latin word meaning 'usual.'

trangam [**tran**-gum] any decorative object which the speaker dislikes.

tranlace [tran-**lace**] to repeat a word in the shape of its cognates or derivatives, especially as wordplay or as a rhetorical device: "My message, my premise, my commission are all the same, and I submit them to you, with my promise, as a missionary, to omit nothing."

transume [tran-**soom**] to make an official copy of a document, usually a legal document.

trental [**tren**-tuhl] thirty requiem masses (said on the same day or on different days) or the payment for saying them. Also, any set of thirty things, or a service said on the thirtieth day after burial. From a Latin root meaning 'thirty.'

trichechine [**trick**-i-kine] an adjective meaning 'like a walrus (or manatee).' It comes from the modern Latin name of a genus (no longer used) including the manatee and walrus, from Greek roots meaning 'having hair.' A good adjective for a particular kind of unfortunate moustache.

trillibub [**tril**-uh-bub] the entrails of an animal, especially in the phrase *tripes and trillibubs* or *tricks and trillibubs.* The etymology of this word is obscure (as are the entrails themselves).

trilling [**tril**-ing] one of a set of three, especially one of a set of triplets; a triplet.

tripotage [**trip**-uh-tahzh] pawing, handling, or fingering, especially of people.

tripudiant [tri-**pyoo**-di-uhnt] dancing; used figuratively to mean 'triumphant, exultant.' The *tripudium* was a ritual dance of ancient Rome, done by armed priests. The dance involved three steps (*tripudium* means 'three feet') and included banging on shields with rods or spears.

tristichous [**tris**-ti-kus] arranged in three rows or ranks. A *tristich* is a group of three lines of poetry or a stanza of three lines; a *distich* is a couplet. They all come from a Greek word meaning 'row.'

troke [trohk]   an obsolete word meaning 'to fail, to be unable to do something' or 'to deceive.' This word comes from an Old English word whose derivation is not known.

tropology [troh-**pah**-luh-jee]   the use of metaphors in writing or speaking. To *tropologize* something is to use it as a metaphor, for instance "He was the John Wayne of the grease pit."

truandal [true-un-**dall**]   a plural noun meaning 'beggars or camp-followers.' From an Old French word meaning 'an assemblage of beggars.'

truchmanry [**truch**-muhn-ree]   the office of an interpreter. The word *dragoman*, meaning 'interpreter,' is related etymologically—they both come from an Arabic word meaning 'interpreter.'

trypall [**trye**-pahl]   a tall, lanky, slovenly person. See **gammerstang**.

tsantsa [**tsahn**-tsuh]   a human head shrunk as a war trophy by the Jivaros of Ecuador in South America. The word comes from the language of this people.

Turlupin [ter-**loo**-pin]   the name for a group of fourteenth-century heretics who believed that one shouldn't be ashamed of anything that is natural. A good word for those who seek to excuse their bad manners or bad behavior with the excuse "everybody does it!"

turngiddy [**tern**-ghid-ee]   an adjective meaning 'dizzy from spinning around.' If you spend too long turngiddy, you might get *turn-sick*, another word for 'dizzy.'

tussy [**tuss**-ee] a decoration or ornament in the shape of a cluster of flowers or leaves, often used as a buckle.

tutoyant [too-twah-**yahn**] an adjective meaning 'intimate, affectionate.' *Tutoyer* means 'to use the familiar pronoun *tu* or *thou*,' or 'to *tu* or *thou* someone.'

tuyere [twee-**yerr** or tweer] the nozzle through which a blast of air is forced into a forge or furnace. It has also been called a *tew-iron* or a *twire-pipe*.

twitter-light [**twit**-er-lite] an obsolete word meaning 'twilight.' It has what to modern ears is an uglier cousin, *twatter-light*.

tykhana [tye-**kah**-nuh] in India, an underground place to rest in during the hottest part of the day. It comes from an Urdu word meaning 'nether house.'

typhlology [tif-**lah**-luh-jee] the scientific knowledge relating to blindness, from Greek *typhlo-*, meaning 'blind,' and *-logy*, meaning 'science of.'

typocrat [**tye**-puh-krat] one who rules by controlling the press. This word was made from *typo-*, meaning 'type,' and the suffix *-crat* on the model of words like *democrat*. A related *typo-* word is *typomania*, the overwhelming desire to see one's name in print.

tyrotoxism [tye-roh-**tock**-siz-um] cheese-poisoning. This particular ptomaine (diazobenzene hydroxide) can also be found in bad milk. From Greek words meaning 'cheese' and 'poison.'

UBIQUARIAN

ubiation [yoo-bee-**ay**-shuhn] the act of occupying a new place. From a Latin word meaning 'where.' *Ubication* is the condition of being in a certain place, and *ubity* is a rare word meaning 'place.'

ubiquarian [yoo-bi-**kwair**-ee-un] a rare word meaning 'a person who goes everywhere.'

ugsomeness [**ug**-suhm-nuhs] a word meaning 'loathing,' which at one time also meant ugliness or 'the quality of being *ugsome*' or horrible. *Uglyography* is an invented word meaning 'bad handwriting or uncouth spelling.'

uliginous [yoo-**lidj**-uh-nus] an adjective meaning 'swampy, slimy, oozy.' From a Latin word meaning 'full of moisture.'

ultra-crepidarian [ul-truh-krep-i-**dare**-ee-uhn] an adjective related to the (widespread) practice of giving opinions on topics beyond one's knowledge. The word comes from Latin words meaning 'beyond the sole (of the shoe),' an allusion to the story of Apelles and the cobbler, Apelles being the favorite painter of Alexander the Great. His shoemaker told him of a mistake Apelles had made in depicting a shoe, and Apelles corrected it. The shoemaker then presumed to criticize the painting of the leg as well, and Apelles said: "Don't criticize above the sole!"

ultrafidian [ul-truh-**fid**-ee-uhn] an adjective meaning 'blindly credulous.' It comes from the Latin phrase *ultra fidem* 'beyond faith.'

umberment [**um**-ber-mint] an obsolete word meaning 'a number, a multitude.'

umbratile [**um**-bruh-tile] an adjective meaning 'spent inside or indoors; private, not public.' From a Latin word meaning 'keeping in the shade.' The noun *umbratile* means 'a person who spends his time in the shade' with the connotation 'lazy.'

umtagati [oom-tah-**gah**-tee] a South African word (from Nguni) meaning 'a wizard or witch; a worker of evil magic.'

undaftiness [un-**daf**-tee-nuhs] untidiness. The word associated with the 'tidy' part is not *daft* 'silly,' but the dialect word *deft*, meaning 'tidy, pretty.'

undern [**un**-dern] an early meaning was 'the third hour of the day' (meant to be about nine o'clock). Later, confusingly, the sixth hour of the day, or midday, and the afternoon or evening. A wonderful word to use when you know you will be late but don't want to admit it: "See you about *undern*!" It can also mean a meal eaten at midday or in the afternoon.

unwelewable [un-**well**-yoo-uh-ble] an obsolete and rare adjective that means 'unfadable.' This word is related to an obsolete *wallow*, meaning 'to fade away, to waste.'

upaithric [uh-**pay**-thrik] an adjective meaning 'having no roof' (usually intentionally, so as to see the stars). A synonym is *hypaethral*, and both words come from a Greek word meaning 'under the sky.'

upbigged [up-**bigd**] a Scots word meaning 'built up.' A more suitable word for strip-mall sprawl could not be found.

UTRICIDE

upbrixle [up-**brik**-sul] upbraid, scold. An obsolete word related to *upbraid*.

uranography [yoo-ruh-**nah**-gruh-fee] a rare and obsolete word meaning 'a description of heaven.' From Greek roots meaning 'heaven' and 'writing.'

usucaption [yoo-zoo-**kap**-shuhn] in law, the acquisition of ownership of a place from having continuous undisturbed or uninterrupted possession. From a Latin law term of the same meaning.

utraquism [**yoo**-truh-kwi-zum] a rare word meaning 'the use of two languages on an equal basis.' From a Latin phrase meaning 'under each kind.'

utricide [**yoo**-truh-side] a person who stabs an inflated vessel of skin. The citations in the *OED* give no clue as to why someone would want to do this (other than to hear the pleasing "pop!"). It comes from a Latin word that means 'a leather bottle.'

uxorilocal [uk-sor-i-**loh**-kul] an adjective meaning 'living in or near the wife's home or community after marriage.' Living near the husband's home is *virilocal*. Another related word is *matrilocal*. It's a synonym for *uxorilocal*, not a word for that butt of frequent jokes, a person living at home with his or her mother.

vagarious [vuh-**gare**-ee-uhs] a rare word meaning 'erratic and unpredictable in behavior or direction.' Its ultimate origin is a Latin verb meaning 'to wander,' and this also gave rise to the English word *vagary*, an unexpected and inexplicable change in a situation or in someone's behavior.

vappa [**vap**-uh] a rare word meaning 'flat or sour wine.' This word has also been used to mean 'a state of the blood when it is in a low, dispirited condition.'

vapulatory [**vap**-yoo-luh-tor-ee] an adjective meaning 'relating to flogging.' Unsurprisingly, it comes from a Latin word meaning 'to be beaten.'

varve [varv] a pair of thin layers of clay and silt of contrasting color and texture that represent the deposit of a single year (summer and winter) in a lake at some time in the past, usually in a lake formed by a retreating ice sheet. The word comes from a Swedish word meaning 'layer.'

vaticinate [vuh-**tis**-i-nate] to predict events; to speak as a prophet. A rarer adjective from the same Latin root is *vaticinant*, meaning 'prophesying.'

vease [veez] a run before a leap. The word is often (well, as often as such a word as this can expect) spelled *feeze* or *pheese*, especially in the United States. A quotation in the *OED* from 1675 reads "If a man do but goe back a little to take his feeze, he may easily jump over it."

veilleuse [vay-**ooz**] a small and highly decorated nightlight. Also, for those fond of midnight snacks, a bedside food-warmer.

verdugoship [ver-**doo**-go-ship] an obsolete word meaning 'the personality of an executioner.' A *verdugo* is a hangman or executioner. The word comes from Italian *verduco,* meaning 'a narrow-bladed sword.'

verecund [**vare**-i-kund] an adjective meaning 'shy, coy, bashful.' Other words that end in -*cund* are the familiar *fecund,* 'fruitful,' *irecund,* 'passionate, angry,' and *namecund,* 'famous.' However, these words are not closely related etymologically. A word that is related to *verecund* etymologically is *vergoynous,* 'ashamed.'

vermian [**ver**-mee-uhn] a rare adjective meaning 'worm-like,' based on the Latin word for worm. Related words in English include *vermicide,* a substance that is poisonous to worms, and *vermivorous,* feeding on worms.

vernicle [**vur**-nuh-kul] the image of Christ's face said to be impressed on Saint Veronica's handkerchief, or any similar image on another item, used for devotional purposes. *Vernicle* is an alteration of *Veronica.*

verticordious [ver-ti-**kor**-dee-us] an obsolete and rare word that means 'turning the heart from evil.' From a Latin word meaning 'turner of hearts,' used as an epithet for Venus.

viduous [**vid**-yoo-uhs] a rare adjective meaning 'empty.' William Makepeace Thackeray (1811–1863) uses this word to describe a heart as a 'viduous mansion' for rent after the loved one is gone, going on to say that the new tenant finds a miniature, or portrait, of the first love hidden away somewhere within it.

vigenary [vi-**jen**-uh-ree] an adjective meaning 'of or relating to the number twenty.' From the Latin word for 'twenty.' A *vicenary* was a person who commanded twenty other people.

vigoro [**vig**-uh-roh] an Australian team game for women, with elements of baseball and cricket, played with a soft rubber ball.

viliority [vi-lee-**or**-i-tee] a rare word meaning 'the fact of being cheaper or of less value.' From a Latin root meaning 'to make viler.'

vimineous [vi-**min**-ee-uhs] a rare adjective meaning 'made of wicker.' From a Latin word meaning 'willow.'

vindemy [**vin**-duh-mee] the taking of honey from beehives. From a Latin word meaning 'fruit-gathering.'

viron [**vye**-run] an obsolete word meaning 'to go around, to make the circuit.' Useful as another word to mean 'going in circles.' From an Old French word meaning 'to turn.'

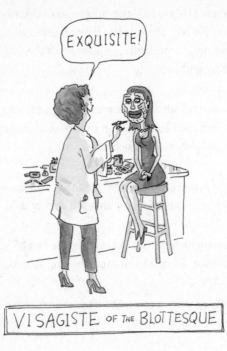

VISAGISTE OF THE BLOTTESQUE

visagiste [vee-zuh-**zheest**] a makeup artist. From a French word with the same meaning.

visceration [vis-uh-**ray**-shun] a rare word meaning 'a portion of raw flesh, especially one distributed at the death of a rich man.' It's assumed that the flesh is that of an animal, and not that of the rich man. Related to the word *viscera*.

viscerotonic [vis-uh-roh-**tah**-nick] having a sociable, easy-going, comfort-seeking personality, usually associated with an endomorphic body type.

voculation [vock-yuh-**lay**-shun] a rare word meaning 'correct pronunciation and enunciation, giving every word its correct accent, moderation, and measure.' From a Latin word meaning 'little voice.' Also from this Latin word is *vocule*, the faint final sound heard when pronouncing certain consonants.

voisinage [**voy**-zin-ij] an obsolete word meaning 'neighborhood,' related to *vicinity*. It can also mean 'the fact of being near,' usually applied only to places, but ready for an extended figurative meaning such as "He was overcome by the *voisinage* of his beloved."

volacious [voh-**lay**-shus] suitable for flying. Something that has the power of flight is *volitorial*. From a Latin word meaning 'to fly.' With the heightened awareness of security in airports lately, this word might come in handy.

volpone [vahl-**poh**-nee] a cunning schemer, a miser. From the name of the main character in Ben Jonson's (1572–1637) play *Volpone, or the Fox* (1606), in which Volpone himself says "What a rare punishment / Is avarice to itself." *Volpone* is an Italian word for 'fox.'

vomer [**voh**-mer] a small bone that is part of the partition between the nostrils in humans and most vertebrates. From a Latin word meaning 'plowshare.'

Vorführeffekt [vor-**fyur**-ef-**ekt**] a German word, literally 'presentation effect' which describes a problem, usually with a computer, that doesn't happen when other people try to replicate it (such as, say, the Help Desk guy you called for).

voulu [voo-**loo**] an adjective meaning 'contrived, affected, deliberate.' The word comes from a French word meaning 'to wish, to want,' and it seems to have had a vogue in the early part of the twentieth century, used by such writers as Elizabeth Bowen (1899–1973) and Lawrence Durrell (1912–1990).

vug [vuhg] a cave, or a cavity or hollow in a rock. The adjective *vuggy* means 'full of cavities.' *Vug* is a Cornish mining term.

Vusvusim [vus-**vus**-eem] a jocular nickname used by Sephardic Jews to refer to Ashkenazic Jews. From German *Was? Was?* 'What? What?'

wabbit [**wob**-it] a Scottish word meaning 'exhausted or slightly unwell,' as in "I'm feeling a bit *wabbit*." Its origin is uncertain.

waff [waf] a Scottish word meaning 'a slight blow, as in passing' or 'a slight touch of illness.' A very useful word, it can also mean 'a glimpse,' 'a wraith,' 'a whiff of perfume,' and 'a waving movement of the hand or something held in the hand.'

wahala [wuh-**hah**-luh] (in Nigeria) inconvenience, trouble, fuss, calamity. From Hausa.

wavenger [**way**-vin-djer] an obsolete word meaning 'a stray animal.' Possibly from *waif*, with the ending modeled after the *-enger* of *passenger, scavenger*, etc.

weddinger [**wed**-ing-er] a wedding guest; also, the entire wedding party, including the bride and groom.

weesle [**wee**-zul] a very rare, undeservedly obsolete word meaning 'to ooze.'

whelve [whelv] an obsolete word meaning 'to turn something over and hide something beneath it' or 'to bury something.' To *whelve over* is to overwhelm.

BOGGLISH WAVENGER

whigmaleery [whig-muh-**leer**-ee] a Scottish word for any whimsical thing or fanciful notion.

whistness [**whist**-nis] an obsolete word meaning 'silence.' Of onomatopoeic origin, related to *hush!* and *hist!*

widdendream [**wid**-un-dreem] an obsolete Scottish word meaning 'in a state of confusion or mental disturbance,' often in the phrase *in a widdendream*. From an Old English phrase meaning 'in mad joy.'

widdiful [**wid**-i-full] someone who deserves hanging. Another word with this meaning is *waghalter*. From *widdy*, 'a rope for hanging.'

windlestraw [**win**-dle-straw] a tall, thin, unhealthy-looking person.

winebibber [**wine**-bib-er] a person who habitually drinks a lot of alcohol. The word was coined by Miles Coverdale (1488–1568) in his translation of the first complete printed English Bible: "Kepe no company with wyne bebbers and ryotous eaters of flesh" (Proverbs 23:20). It is rarely used today except for humorous effect.

winx [wingks] an obsolete word meaning 'to bray like an ass.' If you'd rather sound like the other laughing animal, the hyena, the word for making that sound is *hau-hau*.

woofits [**woo**-fits] an unwell feeling, especially a headache; a moody depression; a hangover. In one citation this is called "that dread disease that comes from overeating and underdrinking" and "the ailment that comes with 'the morning after the night before.'"

wootz [woots] a kind of very tough and sharp steel made in southern India by fusing magnetic iron ore with material containing carbon. Apparently this is a misprint for *wook*.

worble [**wor**-bul] an obsolete Scottish word meaning 'to wriggle or wallow.' Its origin is obscure but it may be related to the word *wrabble*, which also means 'to wriggle.'

woup [woop] an obsolete Scottish word for a ring made of plain metal, without precious stones. *Wup*, a related word, means to bind something together with cord.

wurp [wurp] an obsolete word meaning 'a stone's throw.'

xenization [zen-i-**zay**-shuhn] a rare word meaning 'the fact of travel-ing as a stranger.' It comes from a Greek word meaning 'to entertain strangers' or 'to be a stranger.'

xenelasy [zen-**ee**-luh-see] a law in ancient Sparta by which foreigners could be expelled at any time. The classical city-state equivalent of "the management reserves the right to refuse service to anyone." From Greek words meaning 'foreigner' and 'drive away.'

xenology [zuh-**nah**-luh-jee] the scientific study of extraterrestrial phe-nomena. Mainly used in science fiction, the term comes from a Greek word meaning 'strange': other English words that are based on this root include *xenophobia*, the intense or irrational dislike or fear of people from other countries, and *xenotransplantation*, the grafting or transplant-ing of organs or tissues between members of different species.

xenomenia [zen-oh-**mee**-nee-uh] a medical condition in which blood flows from some part of a woman's body at a different place than (but at the same time as, and replacing) her regular menses. Also called 'vicarious menstruation.' From Greek words meaning 'strange' and 'menses.'

EXCEPTIONAL AND
EXTRAORDINARY X-ES

X the unknown, *X* the mysterious, *X* the secret factor, *X* marks the spot . . .
there's something about a word that starts with X that demands a second
glance. And maybe a third, with some surreptitious scribbling to make sure
you've got the spelling right.

Because X is rarer than we'd like, quite a few of the snazziest X-words
revolve around just a few roots. *Xantho-*, from a Greek word meaning 'yellow,' is one of them. There are the *Xanthochroi*, one of Thomas Henry
Huxley's (1825–1895) varieties of humanity, with their smooth yellow hair
and pale complexions—also called *xanthous*.

Xeno/a- is another one of these roots, from a Greek word meaning 'foreigner,' 'stranger,' or 'guest.' There's *xenagogue*, a fancy word for 'tour guide,'
and *xenagogy*, a fancy word for 'guide book.' A *xenodochium* is a hostel,
especially one in a monastery, and *xenodochy* 'hospitality' is what you
would expect to find there. *Xenization* is the act of traveling as a stranger.
Something that is *xenogeneic* is descended from an individual of a different
species—pretty handy for those long discussions of the consequences of
alien abductions.

A scientific root meaning 'dry,' *xero-*, is also Greek, and shows up in
several X-words, including *xerophagy*, 'the eating of dry food, especially as
a form of fasting,' and *xerotine siccative* 'a substance used to dry ships'
bottoms' (presumably from the inside). Those dry bottoms were probably
made of wood, and wood also has an *x*-root, *xylo-*. *Xylography* is wood-

engraving, especially of the cruder sort, or printing from wood blocks. Something that is *xylophagous* eats wood, like some insect larvae, or destroys wood, as some mollusks do. A *xoanon* is a crudely shaped image or statue of a deity, often made of wood, but it is related to the Greek root for 'scrape, carve,' like *xyster,* an instrument for scraping bones (used in a surgical, not a culinary, way). Once the bones are scraped, you could subject them to *xesturgy,* the process of polishing. You could then wrap the whole thing up in *xilinous* bandages—ones made of cotton.

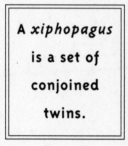

A *xiphopagus* is a set of conjoined twins linked by a band of tissue extending from the *xiphoid* cartilage. Both of these words come from a Greek word meaning 'sword.'

> A *xiphopagus* is a set of conjoined twins.

X can also stand for any number of things, such as the well-known Roman numeral, the *XXX* movie, and the algebraic unknown, but also as *xr,* 'December,' *x* 'ten-dollar bill' and *XX* 'twenty-dollar bill.'

One last note about the letter we call "ex"—the Romans called it "ix" instead. Either way, it's excellent.

xesturgy [**zes**-ter-jee] an obsolete and rare word meaning 'the process of polishing.' From a Greek word meaning 'to polish.'

xu [soo] a monetary unit of Vietnam, formally abandoned in 1986, equaling one hundredth of a dong. The word comes from the French *sou*.

xylophory [zye-**lah**-fuh-ree] a rare word meaning 'wood-carrying,' from a Greek word with the same meaning. The Feast of Tabernacles is a Jewish holiday that used to be called the *festival of xylophory* (now called *Sukkot*), which is celebrated by building a *sukkah* (a ceremonial temporary shelter) in which all meals are eaten for the seven days of the festival. The roof of the sukkah is supposed to be made of something that grew from the ground and was cut off, usually branches (or any wood), corn, or bamboo.

xylopyrography [zye-loh-pye-**rah**-gruh-fee] the art of creating designs on wood with a hot poker or wire. (The word "art" here should probably be in quotation marks, or at least read with air quotes.) A marvelous way of intentionally ruining perfectly good furniture.

yaffle [**yaf**-ul] an English dialect name for the green woodpecker. It originated in the late eighteenth century, apparently in imitation of the bird's characteristic laughing call; in some parts of Britain it's also known as a *yaffingale*.

yaply [**yap**-lee] an adverb meaning 'eagerly, hungrily.' *Yapness* is a noun meaning 'hunger,' and *yap*, obviously, means 'hungry.'

yemeles [**yeem**-lis] an obsolete word meaning 'careless, negligent.' To *take yeme* is to observe or be careful.

yerd-hunger [**yurd**-hung-ger] an overwhelming desire for food, sometimes found in people near death.

yesterfang [**yes**-ter-fang] something that was caught or taken yesterday.

yisel [**yiss**-ul] an obsolete word meaning 'a hostage.'

youf [yowf] to bark in a muffled way.

zabernism [**zab**-er-niz-um] an obsolete word meaning 'to abuse military power or authority, unjustified aggression.' From the name *Zabern*, the German name for Saverne in Alsace, where in 1912 an overeager German subaltern killed a cobbler who smiled at him.

zedonk [**zee**-donk] the offspring of a male zebra and a female donkey, if such a pair is allowed to express their forbidden love. It is also known as a *zonkey* or *zeedonk*, and citations suggest one was born in the (obviously open-minded) Prospect Park Zoo in Brooklyn, New York, in 1973.

zeitgeber [**tsite**-gebb-er] a cyclical event in the environment, especially one that acts as a cue for biological rhythms in an organism. From German words meaning 'time' and 'giver.'

zendik [**zen**-dik] a person "in the East" who not only doesn't believe in the accepted religion, but who has also been accused of "magical heresy."

zenocratically [zee-nuh-**krat**-ik-lee] with the the authority of Zeus or Jove.

zetetic [zi-**tet**-ik] a rare word meaning 'proceeding by inquiry or investigation.' It comes from a Greek verb meaning 'to seek.'

ziraleet [**zi**-ruh-leet] an expression of joy by a group of women in Aleppo, consisting of the words "Lillé, Lillé, Lillé" repeated as often as possible in one breath. Also used figuratively for any expression of joy.

zizany [**ziz**-uh-nee] an obsolete word meaning 'a harmful weed,' also used figuratively in the sense 'a bad apple (that spoils the barrel).'

zoilist [**zoy**-list] a critic, especially one who is unduly severe or who takes joy in faultfinding. From the name of Zoilus (c.400–c.320 BC), an ancient Greek who managed to criticize both Homer and Plato.

zoonosis [zoh-uh-**noh**-sis] a disease transmitted to people by animals, such as rabies. From Greek words meaning 'animal' and 'disease.'

zopissa [zoh-**pi**-suh] a medicinal preparation made from wax and pitch scraped from the sides of ships: fortunately the substance is no longer in use, so the word is obsolete. It came from a Greek word for pitch, a sticky resinous substance obtained from tar or turpentine.

Zyrian [**zi**-ree-uhn] a former term for Komi, a language spoken by a people living in an area of northern Russia west of the Urals. This is currently the last entry in the *OED*.

HOW TO CREATE YOUR OWN
WEIRD AND WONDERFUL WORDS

Every word in English had to start with a person trying to express a thought. As far as we know, none of the words in the English language were brought to the planet by aliens, borrowed from dolphins or whales, or dug up on ancient tablets of unknown provenance. Each and every word was first spoken or written by a person who had to create the word from their own store of sounds and roots.

In almost every case, that inventive person is anonymous. Most words were probably independently created by many different people over a wide area, and can't be traced to a particular writer or speaker. There are some exceptions: Gelett Burgess is said to have coined the word *blurb* 'a short description of a book or other product used for promotional purposes.' *Hotsy-totsy* 'just right' was coined in 1926 by Billie De Beck, an American cartoonist. *Nylon* was coined by DuPont chemists. And *yester-year,* which sounds ancient, was actually coined in 1870 by Dante Gabriel Rosetti, who needed it to aptly translate a French word.

The great majority of coined words, however, are for scientific and technical things. If you have created, discovered, researched, found, developed, or simply predicted the existence of a thing or idea, naturally you'd like to name it. Thus we have the chemical elements *neptunium* (from the planet Neptune: neptunium is just after uranium in the periodic table and Neptune is just after Uranus) and *rubidium* (from a Latin word meaning 'red' because it has red lines in its spectrum). We have tiny organisms, such as *Salmonella* and *rickettsia* (both named after people—Ricketts died because of his work with these parasites) and bigger organisms, like the *allosaurus* (whose name means 'other lizard') and the *Cnidaria* (whose name comes from a Greek word meaning 'nettle,' and oddly enough, they sting!). There are specialized terms in the social sciences, like *etic* (coined by the phoneticist Kenneth Pike, to describe a generalized approach to the structure of language) and *intertextual* (coined by Julia Kristeva: 'denoting literary criticism that considers a text in the light of its relation to other texts'), *subliminal* (coined in the early 1800s, 'below the threshold of sensation or consciousness') and *amusia* (which sounds funnier than it actually is: 'condition in which there is the loss of a musical ability'). *Ornithopter, oogonium,* and *drogulus* are other examples of weird and wonderful coined words. (Determining their meanings is left as an exercise in dictionary use for the reader.)

By this time, you're probably itching to jump in and do a little coining yourself. Although English has no Committee or Academy or Board that reviews new words for suitability and usefulness, there are a few loose rules that tend to work on their own either for or against the widespread adoption of a new word.

The first of these loose rules is unwritten, but not unspoken. It's the rule of pronounceability. Sure, *xzyqt* looks grand, but how do you say it? Be sure to include plenty of vowels in your coinages. Also, it's a good idea to make sure that contiguous consonant sounds are easy to say together. *Adtim* is certain to be pronounced "adim" or "atim," because it's very difficult to correctly enunciate a *d* followed by a *t* and keep them both separate. A handy chart of the sounds of English and the various ways they can be spelled appears on the opposite page.

Sound	Possible Spellings	Sound	Possible Spellings
æ	hat, plaid, calf, laugh, Cheyenne	n	nod, banner, knot, gnat, pneumatic
ā	page, maid, day, freight, skein, hey, steak, valet, straight, gauge, café, soiree	NG	strong, pink, meringue, handkerchief
ä	father, heart, ah, balm, guard, yacht, baa, encore, reservoir, lot	ō	only, goal, grow, soul, doe, brooch, dough, folk, chateau, oh, chauffeur, owe, sew, Seoul, depot, apropos
b	bed, babble		
CH	church, suture, patch, digestion, righteous, cello, Czech, catsup	ô	fall, audio, law, fought, talk, caught, cough, awe, Utah, broad
d	dad, milled, odd		
e	mend, dread, many, said, friend, jeopardy, says, heifer, bury	oi	oil, toy, buoy, lawyer
ē	equal, funny, eagle, tree, ski, believe, either, key, algae, Phoenix, people, buoy, debris	o͝o	pull, wood, amour, wolf, could, Rwanda
er	care, pair, aerial, there, prayer, their, bear, heirloom	o͞o	mood, mule, prove, pooh, group, sue, pew, suit, canoe, maneuver, through, adieu, buoy, debut, coup
ə	occur, about, April, mother, cautious, circus, oxygen, bargain, dungeon, tortoise, pageant, aurora	ow	pout, fowl, bough, hour, Saudi, Mao
f	fan, giraffe, graph, tough	p	pan, happen
g	get, giggle, rogue, guess, ghoul, exist	r	rat, marry, wrath, rhyme
h	her, whole, Gila monster, jicama, Oaxaca	s	sat, cement, dense, trance, kiss, scene, listen, psycho, blitz, sword
i	fin, elastic, gym, manage, ear, guild, sieve, busy, women, marriage, been, weird	SH	short, station, social, fission, tension, machine, tissue, ocean, schwa, sure
ī	ice, fly, pie, high, rye, sign, eye, island, height, either, bayou, kaiser, aisle, aye, guy, Cheyenne, coyote, annihilate, guide	t	tent, matter, stopped, debt, two, thyme, pterodactyl, pizza
		TH	thin
		TH̲	there, breathe
j	jar, gent, charge, fudge, legion, gradual, badge, soldier, exaggerate	v	vest, pave, of
		w	win, wheat, quit, choir, croissant, Nahuatl
k	kin, cup, tack, chemist, ache, account, excite, quick, opaque, liquor, lacquer, Sikh, saccharin	y	yet, onion, accuse, hallelujah, azalea
l	let, bell, tale, pedal, tunnel, lentil	z	zip, musician, fuzz, scissors, ruse, xylophone, clothes, raspberry, asthma, czar
m	men, summon, palm, limb, damn, paradigm	ZH	vision, treasure, massage, azure, regime, equation, nausea

Choose your sounds wisely, then choose the spelling of them. Avoid spellings that have too many possible sounds. Consider *mallough*: is it "maloo" or "maluff"?

You may also want to consider using a simple spelling as opposed to a more complicated or fancy one. No one likes a silent letter, even when deployed for humorous or allusive reasons. (Old joke: Q: how do you pronounce Hen3ry? A: Hen-ree.—The "3" is silent.) If your word is too difficult to spell, people will avoid it out of fear or irritation. Tied in with spelling is the ease of writing the word conventionally. If your word has internal punctuation (such as *ca!met* or *we?zem*) you can pretty much forget about seeing it used widely. (These characters also present a pronunciation problem.) This also applies to inventing your own alphabetic characters. Very few people will want to add a new character to their font sets just to be able to use your new word.

One way to get around spelling and pronunciation problems is to co-opt an existing word and give it a new meaning, rather than attempting to achieve a novel arrangement of letters and sounds. This is how much slang is made. *Lettuce, dough, bread*—all can mean 'money,' now. Inventing slang is a little beyond the scope of this essay. However, if you're determined to create an entirely new word and have thought about the pronunciation and spelling pitfalls, here are a few easy steps.

1. Decide whether you care if your word is *macaronic* or not. A macaronic word takes parts from two or more different languages: a Latin root and a Greek suffix, perhaps. In the word-coining world, a little more credibility is given to words that take all their parts from just one language. They're seen as more sincere.

However, this isn't a hard-and-fast distinction, and it is one that you can safely ignore if you're not inclined to be a purist.

2. Either choose your meaning and look for parts, or choose your parts and look for meaning. Either way, there's a handy list of roots, suffixes, and prefixes here for you to use. If you're dying to have a new word that means "overly eager to speak" you might look for roots *acer* 'fierce, eager' and *dicto* 'to speak', and then add a suffix that makes adjectives, like *-ous*, to get *acerdictous*. (Take care that your suffixes correspond to the part of speech you want. *Acerdictous* doesn't sound like a noun, so it would be odd in: "His *acerdictous* is annoying.") If you are fond of the parts *bathy-* 'relating to depth' and *-ster* 'a person engaged in or associated with a particular activity or thing' you might be tempted to fiddle around until you got *bathyster* 'a particularly deep person.' If you don't find parts for the meaning you want, find a dictionary with good etymologies and look up words that have meanings close to the meaning you want. Avoid ordinary words. For instance, if you're looking for a part that means 'angry,' don't look up *angry*. Look up *irate*. That gets you the Latin root *ira* 'anger.' Can't think of a fancier word for what you want? Use a thesaurus.

3. Don't feel as if you have to use Latin and Greek roots. You may have just as much success merging "ordinary" words. *Humongous* (probably from *huge* and *monstrous)* and *ginormous* (*gigantic* + *enormous*) are two similar and fairly recent words that are rearrangements of other more ordinary words, instead

of meldings of Latin and Greek roots or blendings of roots plus ordinary words.

4. Be practical. It's easier for a new word to gain acceptance if it denotes something for which we don't already have a handy word. Trying to convince people to use your word *kwillum* 'wall' when we already have the word *wall* is a lost cause. If *kwillum* means 'wall being fought over by neighbors' you have a better chance.

5. Once you have a word, try it out on a few people. (I suggest trying it out with your family and friends before unleashing it on your boss or teachers.) Practice saying it several times by yourself. If the pronunciation doesn't come trippingly off your tongue, add sounds where necessary. English is pretty forgiving of the 'uh' sound (often called schwa, represented by ə) and can insert it almost anywhere. Can't say *dreklistic* easily? Try *drekilistic*. Use your new word in informal letters and e-mail and particularly in appropriate postings to Internet forums. If by chance you have the opportunity to be published in traditional media, weigh it carefully as a means of word dissemination. Make sure that the published piece is the right setting for your new word, in both tone and subject matter. You wouldn't introduce a new scientific term in a humorous essay, and a humorous new word might be somewhat out of place in a report on a new scientific discovery.

6. Be patient. It can take years or decades for a new word to be accepted by a majority of speakers. You may not ever see your creation in a dictionary, especially if it was a word created just for a single use or publication (these are called *nonce-words*, and they don't make it into most dictionaries). The joy of having created a word, a word of your very own, should be enough. Do not send your new word to dictionary editors, unless it has been used in major print sources (not just on the Internet or in local or specialist publications) more than a dozen times, by people other than yourself. Anything less than that isn't worth your time or the dictionary editor's.

One last note before you begin: once you have your new word, you might want to look it up in the largest dictionary you can find (I suggest, of course, the *OED*) and online with one or two search engines. You may find that your shiny new word is in fact sporting a fine patina, having been coined already centuries back, or even last week. Something that can be thought probably has been thought, and quite likely already subjected to logopoeia or verbifaction. Good luck!

FINDING NEW WEIRD AND WONDERFUL WORDS

You're reading your favorite magazine, a new novel, or your local paper, and you come across this sentence: "It was an eerie, crebadative feeling, as if she were being watched." *Crebadative?* you wonder. You check a dictionary (or two, or three) and you don't find it. What you have found is a new word. A classic new word, one that has a completely different arrangement of letters from any other existing word. You understand roughly what it means, from context, but you're not sure, and you file it away in your head as new and unusual. You probably won't write it or speak it yourself, unless you're very playful or adventurous—you don't have a firm grasp on it, and there are plenty of other words in your storehouse that you feel more comfortable with. A little later, perhaps, you read this sentence: "Scientists in Melbourne have discovered a new enzyme responsible for fat digestion, lipafazil." *Lipafazil?* You probably don't check that one at all, slotting it instead into a neat compartment in your brain labeled "science stuff." And you don't use it (unless you yourself are an enzyme-research scientist) because you simply have no need for it.

This kind of new-word-finding experience is what most people think of when they (or if they) think about new words: the unique word appearing out of the blue, especially the unique science or technology word. This kind of new word is often called "coined," and in some cases a particular person can be credited with the invention of the word (as with the word *cyberspace*, which was coined by William Gibson in 1982). Even coined words, though, aren't usually completely original combinations of letters; a combination like *phygrttle* is certainly original, but it looks hard to pronounce and doesn't give readers any clue as to what it means, unlike the word *infomercial*, which is a readily recognizable "blend" of *information* and *commercial*. Many coined words are blended from two already accepted words. One completely original coined word is *googol* ('ten raised to the hundredth power [10^{100}]'), which was invented by the nine-year-old nephew of a mathematician.

However, from the lexicographer's point of view, most new words aren't the careful coinage of a single person, or even the simultaneous independent coinages of several people (which happens more often than you might think, to the frustration of all involved). Many new words are stolen by English from other languages; words like *keiretsu*, from Japanese, or *chicano*, from Mexican Spanish. English is very likely to swipe words for food: *chianti, sauerkraut, tandoori*. Sometimes English, instead of taking the word, just transmutes the foreign word into English. German *Übermensch*, for example, became English *superman*. This is called a *calque* (from the French for 'copy') or a *loan translation*. Occasionally, people will hear foreign or unfamiliar words and reanalyze them to fit them into a more familiar form, making new words. This process is called *folk etymology*, and made words like *cockroach*, from Spanish *cucaracha*, and *woodchuck*, from an Algonquian word often spelled *otchek*. Occasionally this process is more involved, as with *alligator pear*, 'avocado'—given this name because they were supposed to grow where alligators were common.

New acronyms are very common, and occasionally become words whose acronymic origins are all but forgotten by users (words like *scuba*, 'self-contained underwater breathing apparatus', and *snafu*, 'situation normal, all (fouled) up', rarely come across as acronyms today, and the origin of a word like *gigaflops*, where the *-flops* is from 'floating-point operations per second,' is not blatantly acronymic). There is even a recent trend toward making *bacronyms*, words that are made acronymically but for which the most important consideration is that the acronym make an appropriate (usually already existing) word or phrase, such as *MADD*, 'Mothers Against Drunk Driving,' or the recent *USA-PATRIOT* Act, in which USA-PATRIOT stands for 'Uniting and Strengthening America by Providing Appropriate Tools Required to Intercept and Obstruct Terrorism.'

Although entirely new words are exciting to the lexicographer and the layperson alike, changes to existing words can thrill as well. The meanings of words are no more fixed than any other aspect of human culture, and despite well-meaning efforts by many to make them stand still, they continue to change. Spotting these new meanings takes a more sophisticated approach to language, and one that is more sensitized to shades of definition instead of just knee-jerkishly categorizing a new meaning as "wrong."

A favorite kind of lexical change is metaphorical extension: the computer meanings of *mouse* and *virus* are good examples of this, as is the basketball meaning of *dunk*. An unfavorite, though frequent, kind of lexical change is change in grammatical function, for example the verbing of nouns. Why one kind of change is welcomed and thought clever by logophiles while the other kind is deplored and thought degrading is unclear, but *impact, contact, script, conference,* and other verbs-from-nouns are in very frequent use.

Words' meanings can get worse, a process called *pejoration;* this has happened in a big way to words like *barefaced*, which originally meant just 'open, unconcealed', and then became 'shameless', and in a small way to words like *poetess* and *actress*, which now seem like lightweights compared to *poet* and *actor*. Words can also improve their meanings, or *ameliorate*. The word *luxury* originally meant 'lust', but gradually changed to mean 'something desirable but not indispensable'.

Besides getting better or worse, meanings can become more or less inclusive. Becoming less inclusive is called *specialization,* as when *amputate* went from meaning 'to cut off' to meaning 'to cut off a limb or other part of the body.' Becoming more inclusive is called *generalization,* as when the word *pants* went from meaning specifically 'pantaloons' to meaning (in the U.S. at least) almost any kind of lower-body covering.

Some new words are just shorter versions of old words. These are made either through *clipping* (*fax* from *facsimile, exam* from *examination* are standard examples) or from *back formation* (*burgle* from *burglar, bus* from *busboy, edit* from *editor*). This is so common that most people don't register these words as "new" or are astonished to learn that the longer word is older. This is probably because many other new words are formed by *derivation,* that is, by adding affixes to existing words, lengthening them. (*Affixes* are prefixes and suffixes, and, in facetious use only, infixes, which are parts inserted in the middle of words. Infixes are usually only used with obscenities: *abso-frickin'-lutely.*) Words like *ascertainable* and *finalization* are derivatives. Many of the new words added to dictionaries are derivatives, added to the end of existing entries.

Words made from proper names are called *eponyms: sequoia* and *silhouette* are two well-known examples. Using a proper name to stand for something having an attribute associated with that name is called *antonomasia,* and calling someone especially perspicacious a *Sherlock* is one example. When proper names are treated in this way they are very often added to dictionaries and thus count, for lexicographical purposes, as new words. The genericization of trademarks (like *thermos* and *aspirin*) also falls under antonomasia.

One last method of forming new words is *echoing*, or *onomatopoeia*, in which new words are made to resemble real-world sounds, like *bleep*, *bloop*, and *boing!* This might be the most fun way to make new words, but it is also less likely to create words that give off that "new" feel, especially if the sound is familiar.

With this field guide to word formation processes you should now be able to find new words everywhere you look—and possibly create a few yourself.

THE LOGOPHILE'S BIBLIOGRAPHY

A Selection of Oxford Dictionaries and Reference Works

DICTIONARIES

The Oxford English Dictionary. 2nd ed. 20 vols. 1989.

The 500-lb gorilla of the dictionary world, also available online by subscription at http://www.oed.com. Check with your local public library to see if they have a subscription for library cardholders available through the library website.

The New Oxford American Dictionary. 2nd ed. 2005.

The second edition of Oxford's flagship American English dictionary, with an innovative arrangement of definitions in which the more prominent core senses are given first, with related senses arranged in blocks underneath. This allows for a nice overview of constellations of meaning not possible with other dictionaries. Comes with a version of the entire dictionary for your PDA, Treo, or BlackBerry.

The Oxford American Writer's Thesaurus. 2004.

Oxford's largest American English thesaurus, with more than 200 word notes from expert writers to help guide your word choices.

The Concise Oxford Dictionary. 11th ed. 2006.

The classic desk-size dictionary for British English, including the most current words and phrases and scientific and technical vocabulary.

Word Formation features identify complex word groups such as -*phobias*, -*cultures*, and -*ariums*.

The New Shorter Oxford English Dictionary. 5th ed. 2 vols. 2002.
Not just an abridgement of the twenty-volume *OED*, the *Shorter* has its own independent research program. With more than 83,000 quotations, this packs the punch of the *OED*'s literary approach in a more manageable format. Also available on CD-ROM.

DICTIONARIES OF USAGE

Burchfield, R.W. ***The New Fowler's Modern English Usage***. 3rd ed. 1996.
A completely revised and expanded version of the beloved *Modern English Usage* with examples from modern authors such as Tom Wolfe, Saul Bellow, and Iris Murdoch.

Fowler, H.W. *A Dictionary of Modern English Usage*. 2nd ed. 1983
The most-beloved language reference book and the one by which all others are judged. And a darn good read!

Garner, Bryan. *Garner's Modern American Usage*. 2003.
The new edition of the classic, from Oxford's authority for American usage. Not just for the grammar-impaired but useful for anyone who would like to write gracefully and precisely.

OTHER WORD BOOKS

Chantrell, Glynnis. *The Oxford Dictionary of Word Histories*. 2002.
This book describes the origins and sense development of over 11,000 words in the English language, with dates of the first recorded evidence from ongoing research for the OED.

Delahunty, Andrew, Sheila Dignan, and Penelope Stock. *The Oxford Dictionary of Allusions*. 2001.
A guide to allusions most frequently found in literature both modern and canonical. It covers classical myths and modern culture and ranges from "Ahab" to "Teflon," "Eve" to "Darth Vader." Many entries include a quotation illustrating the allusion in use.

Greenbaum, Sidney. *The Oxford English Grammar*. 1996.
A complete overview of the subject, including a review of modern approaches to grammar and the interdependence of grammar and discourse, word formation, punctuation, pronunciation, and spelling.

Hargraves, Orin. *Mighty Fine Words and Smashing Expressions*. 2002.
A guide to understanding the stealthy but important differences between American and British English.

Knowles, Elizabeth, ed. *The Oxford Dictionary of Phrase and Fable*. 2000.
Drawn from folklore, history, mythology, philosophy, popular culture, religion, science, and technology, these alphabetically arranged entries include ancient gods and goddesses, biblical allusions, proverbial sayings, common phrases, fictional characters, geographical entities, and real people and events.

Liberman, Anatoly. *Word Origins (And How We Know Them)*. 2004.
The first book to make the science of etymology accessible for the layperson.

McArthur, Tom. *The Oxford Guide to World English*. 2002.
A fascinating and novel survey of English both as a pre-eminent world language and as an increasingly divergent language.

Onions, C. T. *The Oxford Dictionary of English Etymology*. 1966.
The standard reference for scholars, this dictionary delves into the origins of more than 38,000 words.

Ostler, Rosemarie. *Dewdroppers, Waldoes, and Slackers*. 2002.
A guide to the disappearing slang of the twentieth century.

Wilton, David. *Word Myths*. 2003.
A marvelous debunking, type by type, of the most pervasive and persistent folk etymologies. Everything you know about word histories is wrong!